HANDBOOK

3rd Edition
(Revised)

Donald W. Kemper

E. Judith Deneen

James V. Giuffré

HEALTHWISE
P.O. Box 1989, Boise, ID 83701
(208) 345-1161

A Healthwise® Publication

The self-care guidelines in this book are based on the combined research and recommendations of responsible medical sources and have been reviewed by numerous physicians, nurses, and other health professionals for accuracy and safety. The authors and publishers, however, disclaim any responsibility for any adverse effects or consequences resulting from the misapplication or injudicious use of any of the material contained herein.

First Edition, 1981
Second Edtion, 1984, 1986
Third Edition, 1987
Third Edition (Revised), 1989

ISBN: 0-9612690-7-3
Library of Congress Catalog No.: 83-83437

Printed in the United States of America

Contents

Foreword

Good health at any age relies primarily on what you do for yourself on a day-to-day basis. Staying physically fit, eating well, relaxing and maintaining a positive self-attitude can greatly influence how healthy the rest of your life will be.

The *Growing Younger Handbook* is a basic guide to help older people improve their health. By recommending it to my older patients, I have seen first-hand how effectively the book adds to their health successes. Whether you are 20, 40, 60 or 80 you will find in this book both the information you need to make sound health changes and the encouragement you need to turn those changes into a lifetime habit.

Steven L. Schneider, M.D.
Co-founder, Idaho Wellness Center

Note

The information in the *Growing Younger Handbook* will help most readers 60 and older to improve their health. However, health and health problems are in many ways unique to each person. Should you receive professional advice in conflict with this book, carefully consider the health professional's opinion; your unique history and circumstances can then be taken into account. Ultimately, you must accept the full responsibility for your own health decisions and actions.

Healthwise, Incorporated is a nonprofit organization dedicated to helping people succeed in making positive health changes. In addition to the *Growing Younger Handbook* and support materials for the Growing Younger workshops, Healthwise has developed handbooks and training materials to teach younger families to better manage common health problems in the home. Individuals, clinics or other organizations who would like information about other handbooks and programs should contact Healthwise, Inc., P.O. Box 1989, Boise, Idaho 83701. (208) 345-1161.

Acknowledgments

The *Growing Younger Handbook* and the Growing Younger Program were developed under the joint sponsorship of Healthwise, Inc., and the Boise Council on Aging. Our special thanks to Annette Park and Betty Matzek, who contributed sage advice and practical suggestions which added greatly to the Handbook and the success of the program. The material on sexuality was adapted from material originally developed by Mona Wasow.

Thanks are extended to the Growing Younger Steering Committee and the Health Advice Committee for their review of the drafts for the *Growing Younger Handbook* and their suggested changes, additions and deletions to improve its accuracy and usefulness. Committee members included: Bill Hart, Chairman; Goldah Anderson, Blanche Andrews, R.N.; Mark Araki, Bee Biggs, R.N., N.P.; Beverly Clark, Laura Coleman, R.P.T.; Allen Frisk, R.Ph., M.S.; Nancy Keppler, Pat Marshall, Donald Pape, D.D.S.; Joe Patterson, Vi Pollard, Bruce Pyeatt, Bob Richards, Vern Rogers, Clara Ross, Mary Ann Seitz, Bob Vestal, M.D.

Introduction

Have you ever had a friend sixty or sixty-five who looked older and was less active than another friend at 75 or 80? Why do some people "age" faster than others?

Is it because their lives have been hard?

Is it what they eat?

Does it depend on how physically active they are?

Do people age from a lack of love or laughter?

Is aging based on one's genetic heritage?

Does attitude really affect how fast you age?

Do you age more or less because of your doctor's skills or the medicines you take?

Is aging based on how well you can relax?

No one knows how to stop the aging process. But we do know that it's what you do for yourself on an hour-by-hour, day-by-day basis that most determines your health, the way you feel and the way you appear to others.

Growing Younger will provide you with an opportunity to consider how well your day-to-day activities are supporting your health. No one will be asked to give up old habits (though you may be encouraged to try some new ones).

How Can You Grow Younger?

The **Growing Younger** name is based on the fact that a person's health age is not always the same as the actual or birthday age. While you cannot change your birthday age, you can reduce your health age by doing more laughing, walking, relaxing, and good eating. **Growing Younger** can help you do more of those things.

Growing Younger is based on a positive approach to health. And wellness is the positive side of living. When most people think of health, they think of the absence of disease. If they have no signs or symptoms of disease and no disabilities, then they say they are in good health. Under this definition, the best a person could hope for is being free of illness — a neutral state. There is a more positive view of health.

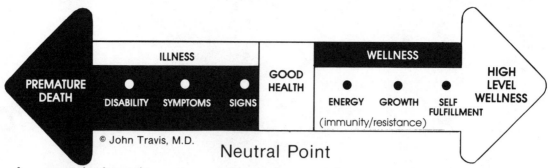

Neutral Point

As people laugh more, walk more, eat better, relax more, and think better of themselves, the benefits they receive are more positive than just avoiding disease.

When people are truly "well," they have an enthusiasm for life that gives them the energy needed to fully enjoy each day.

Growing Younger is planned with equal parts of fact and fun. Fortunately, by learning to feel better, we also become sick less often.

GROWING YOUNGER HANDBOOK

The *Growing Younger Handbook* provides the basic information older adults need to stay active and healthy far longer than most now do. No "miracle cures" are promised. Rather, the book is based on the good common sense of people who have lived long, healthy lives and on the scientific medical research which has backed it up.

The Handbook offers a number of bonuses. In the medical self-care chapter, common health topics from arthritis to constipation are discussed with an emphasis on what the individual can do to prevent, identify and treat each problem. Guidelines are provided on when a health professional should be called.

The personal health care management chapter reads like a consumers' guide to health care. Emphasis is placed on building strong relationships with health professionals in which both parties can communicate effectively and the rights and responsibilities of the individual are recognized. Tips are also included for saving on hospital bills and on getting full benefit from insurance claims.

The *Growing Younger Handbook* is designed for use again and again as new health interests or concerns arise. It should be kept in a handy place at home and referred to before going to doctor visits or starting other health activities. You may write in it and add to it in any way that will help promote your good health.

GROWING YOUNGER, The Program

Growing Younger is also the name of a neighborhood-based health promotion program for older adults which presents and reinforces the good health concepts in this Handbook. Through the program, older adults learn and practice the skills and activities most important to their good health. Even more importantly the program helps people to make and strengthen friendships and to really enjoy themselves.

Growing Younger is organized around neighborhoods so that you can better help each other to stick with whatever changes you decide to make. Our health habits almost always are developed with help from other people. Few people take up smoking without encouragement. Most of us learn to eat what our families and friends eat. Our attitudes toward staying fit usually reflect the attitudes of those around us.

When a person tries to change a health habit such as smoking, overeating, or too little exercise, success usually depends on how much help and support come from family and friends. As people reach retirement age, their neighbors and close friends can become increasingly important to their efforts to improve their health.

By recognizing what changes a friend is trying to make and what barriers might be preventing success, you can learn to lend support in a number of positive and highly effective ways.

When neighbors are involved in the **Growing Younger** program, it encourages stronger friendships and increases opportunities for taking walks together, sharing meals and good times, and generally enjoying good health together.

Growing Younger graduates have shown marked improvements in both how they feel and in what they do. On the average, graduates exercise more often, eat better, relax more completely and feel more competent in managing health problems. These changes have helped participants lose weight and lower their percentage of body fat, as well as reduce cholesterol and increase flexibility.

Growing Younger has led to the creation of senior citizen walking groups (like the Happy Hoofers in Boise), special, older-adult programming at YMCA's, scores of small-neighborhood exercise groups, hordes of service volunteers and many, many other examples of positive, on-going community activities.

While using the *Growing Younger Handbook* can help you achieve many of the individual benefits obtained by participants in the **Growing Younger** Program, just using the book cannot provide the fun, enthusiasm and support usually brought out through the workshops. If **Growing Younger** workshops are available in your community, treat yourself by enrolling. If the workshops are not yet in your town, talk to your hospital, senior citizens center or clinic about sponsoring **Growing Younger** workshops. For more information write Healthwise, Inc., P.O. Box 1989, Boise, Idaho 83701.

Chapter 1
EXERCISE
Use It Or Lose It

In the past few years, Americans have become more aware than ever before of the benefits of exercise and of its importance to total health and fitness for people of all ages. In addition, much attention has recently been given to the role of exercise in improving the quality of life of older people. Age 60 or older can be a wonderful time of life for those who take charge of their physical well-being and maintain the level of fitness necessary for an active, independent life style.

Did you know that **the body's responses to exercise are fundamentally the same throughout life; and that the physical and mental health of older persons who are physically active is significantly better than that of persons of the same age who have led sedentary lives?**

Exercise:

- Maintains fitness
- Stimulates the mind
- Helps to establish social contacts
- Prevents premature dependence on others
- Generally improves the quality of life

The individual who engages in daily exercise is less prone to chronic fatigue than the inactive person regardless of age. Tiredness may be caused by poor circulation resulting from lack of physical exercise. In an inactive person, muscles waste away and bones weaken, reducing strength and endurance. A regular exercise program can build and maintain muscular strength and endurance while also improving the capacity of the heart, circulatory system, and lungs.

> *Regular exercise can change a senior's level of fitness to that of a person 10 to 20 years younger. No matter at what age you begin, or for how long you may have been inactive, exercise will always improve your physical condition.*

The exercise program contained in this handbook has been prepared specifically for persons 60 and over. It is a daily routine of exercise to expand and increase strength, flexibility and endurance.

Strengthening exercises help to build and maintain muscle condition. Muscles become soft, flabby and weak without regular use. This is especially true as we grow older. Simple strengthening exercises are needed to assure your ability to remain active without tiring easily. Muscle strength is needed to support the joints and help prevent arthritic problems.

Flexibility exercises will help you maintain your range of motion. Through the normal aging process, muscles tend to lose elasticity and tissues around the joints thicken. Flexibility exercises can delay or reverse this process by preventing muscles from becoming short and tight. It also helps slow down or prevent development of arthritis. As your range of motion increases, you will be able to reach, turn and move in all directions with more grace and less pain.

*All stretching motions should be done **gradually and slowly,** without any sudden force or bobbing motions. Jerking or bouncing motions can easily pull a muscle and cause an injury. Gradual stretching is safer. Use the full range of joint motion. This may seem difficult at first but with repeated action, your muscles will stretch and flexibility will increase.*

Aerobic or endurance-building exercises strengthen the heart, lungs and blood vessels. Aerobic means "with oxygen" and refers to exercising at a steady rate that requires breathing in more oxygen over a period of time. Brisk walking, cycling, swimming, dancing and jogging are all good aerobic exercises. Practiced regularly, all will strengthen your heart and lungs.

Walking is actually one of the best all-around exercises. The massaging action the leg muscles exert on the veins as you walk improves the flow of blood back to the heart and also strengthens the leg muscles.

Preparing the body for aerobic exercise is important for persons at any age and all fitness levels.

- Do some easy stretching exercises **before** starting your aerobic or endurance activities.

- Begin with a warm-up period of slow, rhythmic activity, like slow walking for a block or so.
- Gradually increase the intensity until your pulse rate, respiration rate and body temperature rise. (See page 6.)

Do not stop your aerobic exercising abruptly. The blood returning to the heart has been assisted by muscle action. **If activity stops abruptly, you may experience blood pooling in the legs. This could lead to mild shock, hyperventilation and even muscle cramping.** Take 5 to 10 minutes to cool down or slow down your activity.

Begin Exercise GRADUALLY!
If you are not accustomed to regular exercise, start slowly and increase your activity very gradually. If at any time you start to feel tired or fatigued, slow down or stop. Overdoing it will only bring sore muscles and joint pain. Be smart about exercise. Starting slowly and sticking with it will bring noticeable results within a few weeks.

UNDERSTANDING YOUR BODY'S RESPONSE TO EXERCISE

You body reacts to exercise in many ways. Some reactions occur as a normal response to exercise. These reactions tell you that your body is adapting to exercise and shaping up.

Normal reactions include:

1. Increased heart rate
2. Increased breathing rate
3. Mild to moderate sweating
4. Feeling or hearing your heart beat
5. Mild muscle aches and tenderness (especially during the first weeks of exercise)

If you have not been exercising on a regular basis, you may find that your balance is not as good as it once was. Many people seem to lose their sense of balance when they are not active. While a regular exercise program can help to maintain or restore balance, care should be taken to avoid falls due to loss of balance.

Other reactions that are **not** normal include:
- Severe shortness of breath
- Wheezing, coughing, or other difficulty in breathing
- Chest pain, pressure or tightness
- Light-headedness, dizziness, fainting
- Cramps, or severe pain or muscle aches
- Severe, prolonged fatigue or exhaustion after exercise
- Nausea
- Joint pain that lasts more than one hour

These reactions may indicate over-exertion, exercising incorrectly, or physical limitations that need to be assessed by a health professional. Learn to "tune in" to your body. As you pay attention to how your body feels, you will soon become your own best guide as to what you can do. If you have been relatively inactive lately, proceed **slowly and gradually.**

Anyone with heart problems, high blood pressure, who is fifty percent overweight, or has been told to be cautious in his activity level, should see a health professional before beginning the exercise program.

KNOW YOUR HEART RATE

Everybody should learn how to take his/her heart rate to monitor both illness and wellness. Your heart rate, also called your PULSE, measures how fast your heart is beating. This rate often changes when you are ill and when you exercise. Everybody has a **resting heart rate** - how many times your heart beats in a minute when you are resting, and not ill. Average rates range from 50-100.

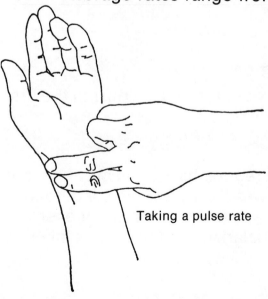
Taking a pulse rate

How To Count Your Pulse - Your pulse can be felt most easily on the thumb-side of your wrist. (A neck pulse will not be as accurate.) Place two fingers over the area with only slight pressure. You should feel a rhythmic beating. Count the number of beats you feel for 10 seconds. Multiply this by 6 to get the number of beats for 60 seconds (one

minute). (You'll need a watch or clock with a second hand.)
Example: 13 beats in 10 seconds gives a one minute pulse of 78 (13 × 6 = 78).

MY RESTING HEART RATE IS _____ .

TARGET HEART RATE FOR EXERCISE

Are you exercising your heart enough? Or too much? You can tell if you are exercising enough to help your heart by learning to take your pulse in connection with exercise.

- **If your pulse is too slow** during exercise, you may not be helping your heart (unless you exercise for long periods at a time).
- **If your pulse is too fast** during exercise, you may be overdoing it and wearing out your heart.
- **If your pulse is in your Target Heart Rate Range** then you are getting the most benefit from exercise.

You may figure your Target Heart Rate from the following chart. **(Circle your target rate.)**

TARGET HEART RATE RANGE

Age	10 Second Target Heart Rate Range	60 Second Target Heart Rate Range
52	17-22	100-134
56	16-22	98-131
60	16-22	96-129
64	16-21	94-126
68	15-20	91-122
72	15-20	89-118
76	14-19	86-115
80	14-19	84-112
84	14-18	82-109
88	13-18	79-106
90 and up	13-17	78-104

Between 60% and 80% of maximal heart rate sets a safe limit for achieving fitness while keeping stress and fatigue to a minimum. (60% is the low number and 80% is the high number in the chart above.)

The target heart rates on page 5 are averages and should be used only as general guidelines. Certainly, if you are taking medication for high blood pressure, you should talk with your physician before setting a target zone for yourself.

THE TALK TEST

Perhaps the best and simplest exercise test is the talk test. If you find that you are exercising so hard that you cannot talk comfortably at the same time, then slow down a little. Of course, if you just talk and stop exercising, it's not going to help much at all.

If you're just starting an exercise program, check your pulse
1. before exercising
2. every 3-5 minutes
3. during your cool-down activities
4. 10 minutes after cool-down. You should be back to your resting heart rate by this time.

If you exercise regularly, check your pulse before, immediately after and 5 minutes after exercising. When exercising, try to maintain your target heart rate for at least 15 minutes. As you get better, extend this time to 30 minutes. Let your body be your guide. If you feel your heart is beating too fast, slow down to a rate at which you feel comfortable.

Whatever you choose to do to reach your target heart rate (walking, bicycling, swimming, running, etc.), make sure you have fun and enjoy it. Do it with a friend or a whole neighborhood of friends.

BEFORE WE BEGIN, A WORD ABOUT THE
IMPORTANCE OF BREATHING

Breathing is a vital part of any exercise program. Often, people who are concentrating on doing an exercise will hold their breath. Learn the correct breathing technique: **breathe out during vigorous effort or exertion** *and breathe in as your muscles relax. Try to establish this rhythm of breathing so that it becomes automatic each time you exercise.*

REMEMBER: Don't hold your breath when exercising.

GETTING UP AND DOWN SAFELY

Some people have a hard time getting down on the floor to exercise. **Follow this procedure to help you get up and down more quickly and easily.**

1.
Stand in front of your chair, bend at the waist with knees bent slightly, and grasp the edge of your chair, supporting yourself. (Make sure your chair is secure and won't slip, and is heavy enough to support you without tipping over.)

2.
Use your arms and the chair to support your weight. Lower one knee slowly and gently to the floor. Do only one knee at a time.

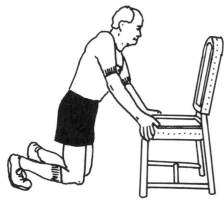

3.
After one knee is firmly on the floor, you can then lower your other knee, but continue to hang onto the chair for support.

7

4.

Hang onto the chair with one hand while you lift your other hand off the chair and place it onto the floor at your right side.

5.

Support your weight with one arm. Bring your other hand over near your body so that both hands and arms support you. Lower your hips gently down to the floor near your hand.

6.

Support yourself with your arms and hands. Lean back slightly, raising one leg straight out in front of you.

7.

Then unfold your other leg and straighten it out alongside the first leg. You should now be sitting on the floor with both legs in front, leaning on your arms.

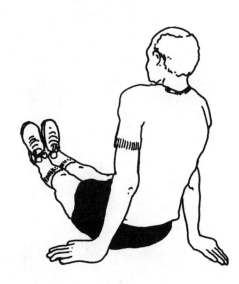

GETTING UP AGAIN

In order to **get up again,** simply get on your hands and knees in front of your chair, Position 3. Then raise your leg up to Position 2. Push up with your arms and legs and slowly stand. At first, practice steps 1, 2, and 3 several times, getting up and down. Then go on to steps 4, 5, 6, and 7. Practice the whole procedure several times in order to become familiar with it.

EXERCISES FOR FLEXIBILITY, STRENGTH, AND ENDURANCE

1. Slow Neck Stretches: To improve flexibility and range of motion of neck. Sit up comfortably. Slowly turn head to the left; return to starting position and slowly turn head to right; return to starting position. Slowly bend head forward until chin touches chest. Suggested repetitions: 2.

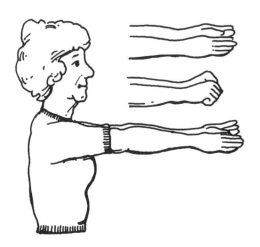

2. Finger Squeeze: To strengthen the hands. Extend arms in front at shoulder height, palms down. Slowly squeeze fingers, then release. Suggested repetitions: 5. Turn palms up, squeeze fingers, release. Suggested repetitions: 5. Extend arms in front, shake fingers. Suggested repetitions: 5.

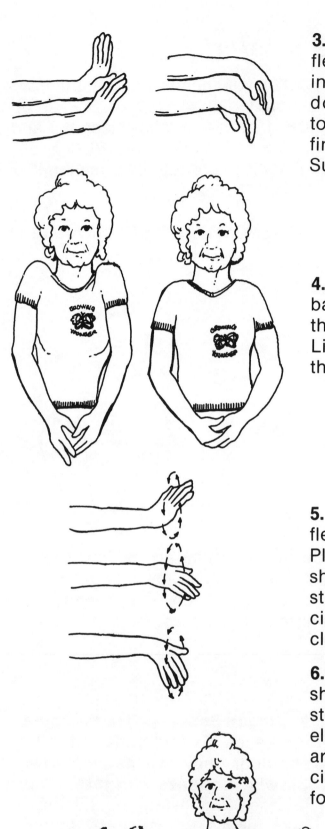

3. Hand Flaps: To increase wrist flexibility and strength. Extend arms in front at shoulder level, palms down. Slowly point fingertips toward ceiling; hold. Slowly point finger tips toward the floor; hold. Suggested repetitions: 5.

4. Shoulder Shrug: For the upper back, to tone shoulders and relax the muscles at the base of the neck. Lift shoulders way up, then relax them. Suggested repetitions: 8-10.

5. Hand Circles: To maintain wrist flexibility and range of motion. Place arms at sides and raise to shoulder level. Keeping elbows straight, rotate wrists in small circles. Suggested repetitions: 10 clockwise, 10 counterclockwise.

6. Arm Circles: To strengthen shoulders and upper back. Sit or stand erect with arms at sides, elbows straight, head high. Rotate arms from shoulders in small circles. Suggested repetitions: 10 forward and 10 backward.

7. Ankle and Foot Circling: To improve flexibility and range of motion of ankles. Cross right leg over opposite knee, slowly rotate foot, making large complete circles. Suggested repetitions: 10 rotations to the right, 10 to the left, each leg.

8. Stretch Tubing Exercises for Strength and Flexibility

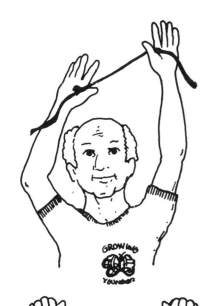

A. Alternate Reach and Stretch: For shoulder, elbow and wrist flexibility. Raise both arms overhead, hands facing forward. Reach for the ceiling with alternate hands. Suggested repetitions: 5 each hand.

B. Overhead Stretch: For arm and shoulder flexibility and strength. Raise both arms overhead, hands facing forward. Pull both arms away from center to tighten tubing; relax. Suggested repetitions: 5.

C. Up-Down Stretch: For arm and shoulder flexibility. Raise both arms overhead; put moderate tension on tubing; bend elbows, lower arms, bring tubing to rest behind head on shoulders. Suggested repetitions: 5.

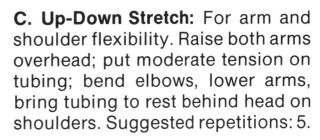

D. Alternate Arm Stretch (Back): For arm strength and elbow flexibility. Place left hand at back of neck. Straighten right arm to stretch tubing tight. Reverse, repeat with left arm. Suggested repetitions: 5 each arm.

E. Chain Breaker: For shoulder flexibility and chest muscle tone. Raise arms to shoulder level, elbows flexed, hands at center of chest. Pull hands apart, stretching tubing. Suggested repetitions: 5.

F. Alternate Arm Stretch (Front): For arm strength and elbow flexibility. Place left hand at center of chest. Straighten right arm to stretch tubing tight. Reverse, repeat with left arm. Suggested repetitions: 5 each arm.

G. Lap Level Stretch: To strengthen lower arms. Drop arms to sides. Pull hands and arms away from body to tightly stretch tubing. Suggested repetitions: 5.

H. Alternate Flat Foot Stretch: To strengthen arm and back muscles. Loop tubing under arch of right foot. Keeping foot firmly on floor, raise your body to an upright sitting position. Reverse and repeat with left foot. Suggested repetitions: 5 each foot.

I. Alternate Straight Leg Stretches: For leg flexibility and arm strength. Loop tubing under arch of foot. As you raise your body to upright sitting position, raise your leg, keeping knee straight. Reverse and repeat with other leg. Suggested repetitions: 5 each leg.

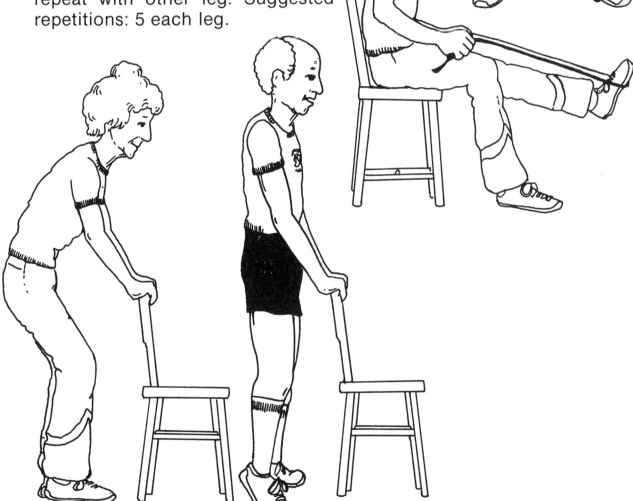

9. Alternating Knee Bends and Heel Raises: To tone and strengthen lower legs and ankles. Stand erect behind a chair; place hands on chair back for balance. Bend knees into a quarter-squat position; raise up on toes; return to starting position. Suggested repetitions: 10.

10. Knee Lift: To strengthen hip flexors and lower abdomen. Stand erect with hand on back of chair (as illustrated). Raise left knee to chest or as far upward as possible. Return to starting position. Suggested repetitions: 5 each leg.

11. Back Leg Swing: To firm the buttocks and strengthen the lower back. Stand erect behind chair, feet together, hands on chair back for support. Lift one leg back and up as far as possible, keeping knee straight. Return to starting position. Suggested repetitions: 10 each leg.

12. The Rocker: To strengthen arms, legs and back. Stand facing other person or wall. Take a comfortable stance with right leg forward (other person puts left leg forward). Extend arms, touching palms and fingers together. Push forward, then back, in a rocking motion. Repeat 5 times. Reverse legs; repeat 5 times.

13. Side-Arm Stretch: To stretch and strengthen chest and arm muscles. Stand in a line. Place arms at sides and lift to shoulder level, touching palms and fingers with person on either side. Push against other person, then relax, allowing the other person to push against you. This can also be done by pushing against a wall. Suggested repetitions: 5 both arms.

14. Side Stretch: For shoulder and flank flexibility. Stand with feet apart for balance. Raise right arm over head, leaving left arm at side. Bend toward the left; reach right arm overhead. Repeat 5 times. Reverse arms; repeat 5 times.

15. Swim Stroke: To stretch shoulder girdle. Stand with feet shoulder width apart, arms at sides relaxed. Bend knees and alternately swing right and left arms backward, upward and forward as if swimming. Suggested repetitions: 6-8 movements on each side.

16. Toe Touches: To maintain flexibility in torso, low back and legs. Stand erect, knees slightly bent, feet shoulder width apart, arms at sides, slowly bend forward as far as possible. Suggested repetitions: 4-6.

17. Sitting Stretch, Legs Together: To stretch lower back and hamstrings. Sit on floor, legs extended forward, knees together. Exhale and stretch forward, slowly sliding hands down to ankles. Touch chin to knees, keeping legs as straight as possible. Hold 5-8 counts. Don't bounce. Return to starting position, inhaling deeply. Suggested repetitions: 3-4.

18. Sitting Stretch, Legs Apart: To increase flexibility of lower back and hamstrings. Sit on floor, legs extended shoulder width apart. Place hands on floor at sides for support. Stretch forward slowly and extend arms between legs. Hold for 3-5 counts. Suggested repetitions: 3-5.

19. Sit-up: To strengthen stomach muscles. Lie on back, knees bent, legs apart, feet on the floor, arms at sides. Curl body upward, lifting shoulders off floor. Uncurl down to starting position while inhaling. Suggested repetitions: 5.

20. Head and Shoulder Curl: To firm stomach muscles and front of neck. Lie on back, legs forward, knees slightly bent, arms at sides. Curl head and shoulders off floor. Hold for 5 counts. Return to starting position. Suggested repetitions: 10.

21. Single Knee Pull: To stretch lower back and back of leg. Lie on back, hands at sides. Pull one leg to chest, grasp with both arms and hold for 5 counts. Repeat with opposite leg. Suggested repetitions: 3-5.

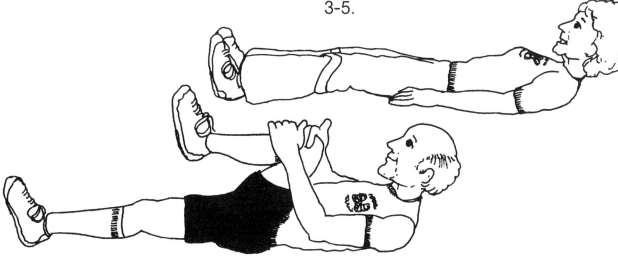

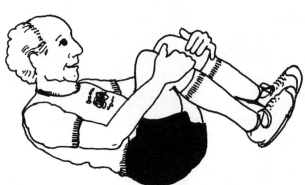

22. Double Knee Pull: To stretch lower back and buttocks. Lie on back, hands at sides. Pull both legs to chest, lock arms around legs, pull buttocks slightly off ground. Hold for 10-15 counts. Suggested repetitions: 3-5.

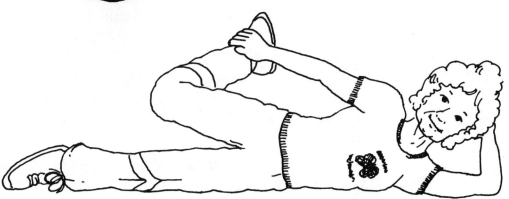

23. Half Bow: To stretch the top of the thigh and groin area. Lie on left side. Grab ankle of right foot with right hand just above toes. Slightly arch back. Hold 5-10 counts. Suggested repetitions: 3-5.

24. Side Lying Leg Lift: To strengthen and tone outside of thigh and hip muscles. Lie on right side, legs extended. Raise left leg as high as possible. Lower to starting position. Suggested repetitions: 10 each side.

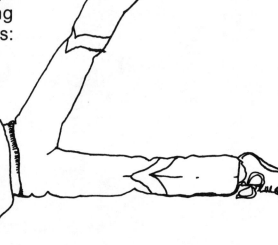

18

25. The Cobra: To stretch abdominal wall, chest and front of neck. Lie stomach down, feet extended with toes pointed. While exhaling slowly, push up on arms and arch back. Hold for 5-10 counts. Return to starting position, inhaling deeply. Suggested repetitions: 4-6.

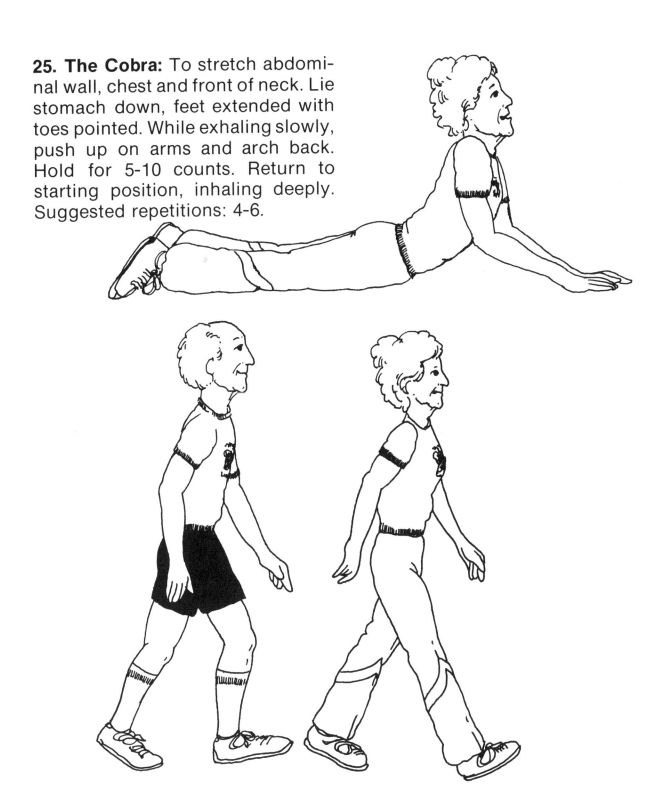

26. Walking For Fun and Fitness. The following walking program has been designed to help you build and maintain heart and lung capacity. Walking offers several advantages over other forms of exercise — it requires no previous instruction; it can be done almost anywhere; it can be done at almost any time, it costs nothing and it has the lowest rate of injury of any form of exercise.

Although walking at any speed is beneficial, the benefits increase dramatically as you increase your pace. To receive maximum benefit, increase your pace until you reach your exercise target heart rate (see page 5). Fast walking also aids in weight control. While walking a mile in 20 minutes will burn off 66 calories, a 12-minute mile will use up 124 calories, almost twice as many.

Brisk walking is a little harder on the joints than slow walking, so gradually build up your pace over a period of several months.

Choose a comfortable time of day to exercise, not too soon after eating and when the temperature is not too high. Follow the program at the recommended rate but be careful not to over-exert. Stop if you find yourself panting, feeling nauseous, if your breathing does not return to normal within ten minutes after exercising or if your sleeping is affected. If you feel uncomfortable progressing at the recommended rate, spend additional weeks at each level of exercise.

WALKING TIPS

A good walking workout is a matter of stepping up your pace, increasing your distance and walking more often. Here are some tips to help you get the most out of walking.

1. **Move at a steady clip,** brisk enough to make your heart beat faster and cause you to breathe more deeply.
2. **Hold your head erect,** back straight and abdomen flat. Toes should point straight ahead and arms should swing loosely at your sides.
3. **Land on your heel** and roll forward to push off the ball of your foot. Walking only on the ball of the foot or walking flatfooted may cause soreness.
4. **Take long, easy strides** but don't strain. When walking up hills or walking rapidly, lean forward slightly.
5. **Breathe deeply,** with your mouth open if that's more comfortable.

WHAT TO WEAR WHEN WALKING

Shoes that are comfortable, provide good support and don't cause blisters or calluses are the only special equipment necessary. They should have arch support and should elevate the heel one-half to three-quarters of an inch above the sole. They should also have uppers made of materials that "breathe" such as leather or nylon mesh. Some examples are: training models of running shoes with thick soles, light trail or hiking boots or casual shoes with thick rubber or crepe rubber soles.

20

Wear lighter clothing than the temperature would ordinarily dictate because walking generates a lot of body heat. In cold weather, wear several layers of light clothing. They trap body heat and are easy to shed if you get too warm. A woolen cap is important in very cold temperatures.

START WALKING - 15 Week Schedule

1st Week and 2nd Week - 3 sessions on alternate days - ¼ mile (2½ blocks). Use good posture and proper walking techniques. Dress comfortably.

3rd Week - 3 sessions on alternate days - ½ mile (5 blocks). Gradually lengthen stride. Practice deep breathing each 220 yards or every 1½-2 blocks.

4th Week - 3 sessions on alternate days - ¾ mile (7½ blocks). Do deep breathing each 220 yards or every 1½-2 blocks.

5th Week - 3 sessions on alternate days - 1 mile (10 blocks). Practice deep breathing each 220 yards or every 1½-2 blocks. Lengthen stride.

6th Week - 5 sessions - 1 mile (10 blocks). Practice deep breathing. Emphasize good posture.

7th Week - 5 sessions - 1 mile (10 blocks) each in 20 minutes.

8th Week - 5 sessions - 1½ miles (15 blocks) each in 30 minutes.

9th Week - 5 sessions - 2 miles (20 blocks) each in 40 minutes.

10th Week - 5 sessions - 2 miles (20 blocks) each in 40 minutes.

11th Week - 5 sessions - 2½ miles (25 blocks) each in 50 minutes.

12th Week - 5 sessions - 3 miles (30 blocks) in 60 minutes.

13th Week - 5 sessions - 3 miles (30 blocks) in 55 minutes.

14th Week - 5 sessions - 3 miles (30 blocks) in 50 minutes.

15th Week - 5 sessions - 3 miles (30 blocks) in 45 minutes.

If you are already an active walker, locate your present distance and speed on the schedule and begin the program from there.

INJURIES CAN HAPPEN

Occasionally during a regular exercise program, you may experience aches, pains, strains, sprains, or other minor injuries. Many such injuries heal by themselves. The most common cause of exercise injuries is over-exertion — pushing yourself too hard, or not preparing by doing inadequate stretching and warm-up activities.

What To Do First

The immediate treatment for most injuries of this type is the same, whether you have pulled a muscle, strained a ligament, hurt a joint, or bruised. It is called the "ICES" Method.

ICE: **Immediately apply ice, or a "cold pack," 20 minutes on, 40 minutes off, every waking hour for the first 24-48 hours after injury.** Cold constricts blood vessels, prevents further swelling, reduces pain and reduces muscle spasm.

COMPRESSION: Compression wrap with 4"-6" Ace bandage. Prevents further swelling, helps support injured area.

ELEVATION: Elevating the injured part above the level of the heart will also help to prevent further swelling.

SUPPORT: Support of the injured area with a sling, crutches, cane, etc. Keeps pressure off injured area and prevents further injury.

Because swelling usually starts within seconds after an injury, start treatment as soon as possible.

Decrease or modify your activity but do **not** discontinue completely. You may continue walking but not as fast or as far until you have healed.

22

If walking is too uncomfortable, try another type of activity for a while.

Foot problems such as blisters or calluses can be avoided by wearing properly fitted shoes with stockings. Some people have found that wearing two pairs of light stockings is helpful in preventing blisters. If you get a blister, keep it clean and don't break or open it. If it breaks, avoid infection by keeping it clean and dry. Never cut or apply strong chemicals to a callus. Calluses are best treated by gently rubbing with a pumice stone, then applying a skin softening lotion.

Bruises may result from bumps or falls caused by walking on an unsafe surface. Certain medications such as anticoagulants (blood thinners), steroids (such as cortisone) or aspirin and aspirin-related drugs may cause you to bruise more easily. In such cases, the immediate use of the "ICES" treatment (page 22) is especially important.

When to See a Doctor
You should consult a physician for:
1. Any injury accompanied by **severe** pain. Pain is nature's way of talking to you and when it speaks loudly, you must listen.
2. Any pain in a joint or bone that persists for more than 2 weeks. These tissues are the ones in which the most serious injuries occur.
3. Any injury that doesn't heal in three weeks. All injuries that don't heal should be checked for a possible break or crack in a bone.
4. Any infection in or under the skin accompanied by pus, red streaks, swollen lymph nodes, or fever. Untreated infections may lead to serious complications.

These guidelines are designed to save you from unnecessary medical bills and perhaps unnecessary treatment. It must be realized, however, that every injury is a happening unto itself and should be treated on its own merits.

MUSIC MAKES IT FUN

Music has a positive effect on both mood and tolerance and is expecially pleasant for people who are exercising. You may enjoy doing the exercises in this book to music. Music, of course, is a matter of individual preference, and the choice is up to you. Waltzes are nice background for flexibility and relaxation exercises, while polkas are great for doing aerobic activities.

SOME POINTS TO REMEMBER

Once you have begun your daily exercise program, keep these points in mind for more satisfying results:

1. *Start gradually, about 5 to 10 minutes at first.*
2. *Wear comfortable clothing.*
3. *Increase the amount of exercise each day, up to about 30 minutes.*
4. *Always do stretching exercises to "warm up" before and "cool down" after aerobic exercise.*
5. *Avoid dizziness by pausing briefly before changing direction.*
6. *Breathe deeply and evenly between exercises and during exercise. **Don't hold your breath.***
7. *Rest whenever necessary.*
8. *Keep a daily written record of your progress, including your resting and exercise heart rates.*
9. *Exercise to lively music, TV or with friends for added enjoyment.*
10. *Make exercising a part of your daily routine.*
11. *While you're exercising, consider the benefits:*
    - *It enriches the blood and improves the circulation.*
    - *It restores elasticity and strengthens muscles.*
    - *It builds endurance.*
    - *It improves the posture.*
    - *It usually improves one's morale and confidence by helping one to feel and look younger.*
    - *It enhances agility and mobility.*
    - *It can be fun.*

THE REST IS UP TO YOU

You have the right to enjoy the benefits of regular exercise. It improves the quality of your life by adding to your health.

Remember, **it is important to begin an exercise program slowly and build up gradually.**

It is never too late to "get fit." Even after years of inactivity, your body will respond positively to regular exercise. Without a doubt, your body is a machine that breaks down when you don't use it. Unquestionably, it works better when you use it.

GOOD BOOKS ON EXERCISE

Dr. Simon J. Winkler, *Walk, Don't Run,* Wendard Pub., Inc., Miami, Fla., 1980

Covert Bailey, *Fit or Fat,* Houghton Mifflin Co., Boston, Mass., 1978

Lawrence J. Frankel and Betty Byrd Richard, *Be Alive As Long As You Live,* Lippincott & Crowell Pub., N.Y., 1980

Kate Lorig and James Fries, *The Arthritis Help Book,* Addison-Wesley Pub. Co., 1980

Travelers Insurance Co., *Pep Up Your Life, A Fitness Book For Seniors,* Hartford, Conn.

Bill Gale, *The Wonderful World of Walking,* Dell Pub. Co., 1979

Alice Christensen and David Ranken, *Easy Does It Yoga for Older People,* Harper & Row, 1979

Chapter 2
RELAXATION
Skills For Relaxation

Like the need for exercise, our bodies have a need for regular relaxation. The fast pace of modern life combined with worries about politics, crime, inflation or illness can keep a person tense and stressed most of the time. Unless we can regularly unlock and release that tension and stress, it can greatly increase our risks of developing heart disease, cancer and other chronic illnesses. Besides that, being relaxed is a lot more fun than being worried, uptight and tense.

Aging and Stress

Stress can make you "age" faster. In people prone to ulcers, stress wears out the stomach. In others, it may damage the heart, lungs, skin or muscles. Few people die of "old age." Instead they die because their hearts and other vital organs just wear out. How fast they wear out has a lot to do with how much stress a person has and how well he or she can deal with it.

Fight or Flight Response (Stress Response)

The human body is magnificently equipped to respond to stress. When we are challenged or threatened, our bodies go through a series of changes which prepare us to either fight the threat or run away from it. This fight or flight response is made up of the following bodily changes:

- Your **heart** beats faster to pump more blood to your lungs, brain and muscles.

- Your **blood pressure** increases.

- Your **muscles** tense to prepare you to fight or run away.

- You **breathe** faster to get more oxygen.

- Your **digestion** slows (butterfly feeling in the stomach) so energy can be used elsewhere.

- You **perspire** more as your body tries to cool itself (sweaty palms).

- Your **skin** turns pale (much of your blood is flowing to your muscles).

- Your pupils dilate (get larger) to allow you to **see** better.

- Your hearing becomes more acute — you **hear** better.

27

- You may experience **strong feelings** as hormones are released which can cause you to feel tension, fear, anger or happiness.
- You may **feel stronger** as more sugar enters the blood stream to be burned more rapidly by your muscles.

When you really need to get away, this stress response is truly a miracle of survival. Today, however, our tensions are most often caused by things such as: time pressures, loneliness, loss of a loved one, or fear of the future (retirement, health, etc.).

Whenever you make an important decision, cope with a difficult situation, or even look forward to an exciting event, your body processes automatically prepare you for action with the stress response. When channeled into productive activities, the stress response motivates you to get things done and helps you deal with unexpected situations. But if you feel stress too much of the time and can't cope with it effectively, your body will be constantly tensed up with no release.

WHAT IS DISTRESS?

Stress isn't bad. Without some stress and change, our lives would be quite boring. Stress only becomes harmful when we let it get out of hand. If we can't fight it, run from it, or react to it in some other positive way, stress can become distress.

Distress occurs when our body is all charged up with no place to go. During distress, the body is like a motor revved and raring to go. When restricted, the energy is bottled up inside you. If this energy is bottled up (repressed) 5, 10, 20 times a week, the body's rate of wear and tear increases. Such chronic distress can eventually result in serious health problems as described below.

Stress-Related Problems and Symptoms

Ulcers .... Stomach pain, "gnawing feeling"

High Blood Pressure ... No symptoms

Arthritis .... Pain in joints or muscle tension

Heart Disease .... Chest pains, difficulty breathing

Cancer .... Increased susceptibility

Headaches . . . . Constant worrying
Circulatory Problems . . Cold hands and feet
Backaches . . . . Muscle spasms or chronic pain

What Causes Stress?

Most of us experience stress from three basic sources.

1. Our **environment** bombards us with stress. Crime, weather, noise, crowding, time pressures, demands of others, pollution and expectations all create tensions which we must deal with on a daily basis.

2. Our **bodies** can cause us stress. Illness, accidents, drugs, lack of sleep, and even the normal process of aging can create stresses which must be dealt with.

3. Our **minds** too, can create stresses. Our attitudes and perceptions largely determine the difference between fear and challenge, boredom and relaxation, despair and hopefulness. Retirement can be either a time to look forward to or a time to dread. If you think about retirement as an opportunity for doing the things you always wanted to do but never had the time for, it will probably be a relaxing stage of life. However, if you worry about financial security, self worth or uselessness, it can be very stressful.

Distress is usually caused by one or more of these stress sources working together. Your body really doesn't care where the stress comes from, it just wants to get rid of it.

Think for a moment about a bad **headache.** The headache can be triggered by noise (your environment), by what you eat or drink (your body), or by intensive worrying about someone you care about (your mind). Although the headache may feel the same, learning what stress caused it is the first step in preventing its return.

Most of us probably underestimate how many stressful events occur each day to which we must adjust. The best way to figure out what causes you stress is to keep a daily journal of stressful situations. Use the following list of common stress symptoms along with the Stress Log on the next pages to help you recognize when you're feeling tension.

```
┌─────────────────────────────────────────────────────────────┐
│                    Symptoms of Stress                         │
│   • Sweaty palms             • Headaches, neckaches,          │
│                                backaches                      │
│   • Shortness of breath                                       │
│                              • Pain or discomfort caused      │
│   • Rapid breathing            by muscle tension              │
│     (hyperventilation)                                        │
│                              • Dry throat and mouth           │
│   • "Butterflies" in the                                      │
│     stomach                  • Clumsiness                     │
│                                                               │
│   • Nervous or shaky speech  • Can't concentrate              │
└─────────────────────────────────────────────────────────────┘
```

Instructions: At the end of each day (for one week) think over your day's activities and write in any time you felt stress or tension; what event caused it; what symptoms you felt; and how you coped or relieved the stress.

STRESS LOG
Journal of Daily Stressful Situations

Day	Time	Stressful Event/Situation	Symptoms	Coping Style

Major Sources of Stress

In addition to the day-to-day tensions of life, we also must deal with major life changes that can greatly increase stress. While the body usually reacts to stress in the same general way, certain life changes can cause much stronger stress reactions than others.

To summarize the degree of stress received from major changes in your life, complete the Life Change Scale which follows. The more changes you have made in the last year, the greater is your risk of stress. Higher levels of stress are associated with greater risk of illness. If your score is high (above 250), don't despair. The regular practice of the stress reduction methods presented later in the chapter can prevent distress from setting in.

LIFE CHANGE SCALE

Think back on each possible life event listed below and decide if it happened to you within the last year. If any of these life events have happened to you in the last 12 months, please enter the life crisis unit in the score column.

RANK	LIFE EVENT	LIFE CRISIS UNITS	YOUR SCORE
1	Death of spouse	100	_____
2	Divorce	73	_____
3	Marital separation	65	_____
4	Jail term	63	_____
5	Death of close family member	63	_____
6	Personal injury or illness	53	_____
7	Marriage	53	_____
8	Fired at work	47	_____
9	Marital reconciliation	45	_____
10	Retirement	45	_____
11	Change in health of family member	44	_____
12	Pregnancy	40	_____
13	Sex difficulties	39	_____
14	Gain of new family member	39	_____
15	Business readjustment	39	_____
16	Change in financial state	38	_____
17	Death of close friend	37	_____
18	Change to different line of work	36	_____
19	Change in number of arguments with spouse	35	_____
20	Mortgage over $10,000	31	_____
21	Foreclosure of mortgage or loan	30	_____
22	Change in responsibilities at work	29	_____
23	Son or daughter leaving home	29	_____
24	Trouble with in-laws	29	_____
25	Outstanding personal achievement	28	_____
26	Spouse begins or stops work	26	_____
27	Begin or end school	25	_____
28	Change in living conditions	25	_____
29	Revision of personal habits	24	_____
30	Trouble with boss	23	_____
31	Change in work hours or conditions	20	_____
32	Change in residence	20	_____
33	Change in school	20	_____
34	Change in church activities	19	_____
35	Change in recreation	19	_____
36	Change in social activities	18	_____
37	Mortgage or loan less than $10,000	17	_____
38	Change in sleeping habits	16	_____
39	Change in number of family get-togethers	15	_____
40	Change in eating habits	15	_____
41	Vacation	13	_____
42	Christmas	12	_____
43	Minor violations of the law	11	_____
		YOUR TOTAL	_____

(Holmes, T.H., and Ruhe, R.H., *Journal of Psychosomatic Medicine,* 1967, 2:213.)

Life Change Score Guide

The more major life changes you've had, the greater is your risk of getting a **distress** related illness. Your score can only tell you about your **chances** of becoming ill. If you have a high score, consider using one of the relaxation activities that follow on a regular basis to prevent an illness.

Score	Risk of becoming ill in near future
0-150	30%
150-299	50%
Over 300	80%

The following suggestions can help you actively use the Life Change Scale to maintain good health and prevent illness during stressful times.

1. Become familiar with the life events so you will recognize when they happen.

2. Think about how each life event affects you and how you might best adjust to it.

3. Take your time in arriving at decisions (don't be rushed by the event).

4. If possible, anticipate life changes and plan in advance how you can deal with the extra stress they bring.

5. Turn the event into a time for positive growth. Look at it as a learning opportunity.

6. Practice a relaxation activity of your choice.

SKILLS FOR RELAXATION

Stress! You have it. What are you going to do about it? You can't escape all of the stresses of life but you **can** learn to relax.

Learning how to relax will help you:

- perform better under pressure
- sleep better
- control your blood pressure
- lower your cholesterol
- reduce or eliminate use of drugs, alcohol and tobacco
- reduce headaches
- relieve depression
- smile more

The relaxation activities described in the following pages include:

- **Breathing Activities -** an immediate way to reduce stress
- **Progressive Muscle Relaxation -** an easy way to relieve muscle aches
- **The Relaxation Response -** a simple meditation procedure to counteract the stress response
- Several **brief relaxation techniques** you can practice any time and anywhere:
  - eye relaxation   - color imagery   - guided imagery

You should find that one or more of these activities are just right for you. Here are some suggestions to get the most out of them:

- Choose a relaxation activity that you find easy to do.
- Keep daily records of your progress (journal).
- In the beginning, when practicing these activities, do at least two times a day (15 minutes each time) for one full week to give them a chance to work.
- Don't expect instant miracles. Try the activity for at least three weeks before expecting to notice results.
- Be creative — make up your own guidelines.
- Lie down in a comfortable position, turn the lights down low, close your eyes, and if you like, play some relaxing background music . . . enjoy.

BREATHING

Breathing is the key to life. Full breathing is a good way to reduce tensions and to feel relaxed. Each breath of air you take has the potential to purify and oxygenate your blood. Oxygen nourishes your tissues and organs and is essential to good mental and physical health. Too often people breathe in short, incomplete breaths that leave stagnant air in portions of the lungs and reduce the flow of oxygen to the blood.

Proper breathing is a learned skill. The breathing activities suggested in the next few pages have been designed to help you relax. After you learn the basic procedures, you can use these exercises to immediately relax. Deep breathing can become your special cue to release tension. It can be a catalyst to slow down all the body processes which are normally elevated during a stress response.

Experiment and adapt until you find the breathing activity which is most comfortable for you.

> *DON'T HOLD YOUR BREATH*
> *Breath holding is a symptom of stress. Whenever you find yourself holding your breath, use it as a cue to take time out to relax.*

Benefits of Breathing (the Relaxing Way)

- Immediate stress reducer
- Life-giving oxygen and energy
- Purifies your blood
- Simple and always available
- Can warm cold hands and feet
- Filters and expels impurities
- Enhances complexion
- Nourishes vital organs
- Very relaxing
- It's still free

ROLL BREATHING

The object of roll breathing is to develop full use of your lungs. It can be practiced in any position but is best learned lying down, with your knees bent.

1. Place your left hand on your abdomen and your right hand on your chest. Notice how your hands move as you breathe in and out.

2. Practice filling your lower lungs by breathing so that your left hand goes up and down while your right hand remains still. Always inhale through your nose and exhale through your mouth.

3. When you have filled and emptied your lower lungs 8-10 times with ease, add the second step to your breathing: Inhale first into your lower lungs as before but then continue inhaling into your upper chest. As you do so, your right hand will rise and your left hand will fall a little as your stomach is drawn in.

4. As you slowly exhale through your mouth, make a quiet, relaxing whooshing sound as first your left hand and then your right hand falls. Exhale, and feel the tension leaving your body as you become more and more relaxed.

5. Practice breathing in and out in this manner for 3-5 minutes. Notice that the movement of your abdomen and chest is like the rolling motion of waves rising and falling in a rhythmic motion.

Roll breathing should be practiced daily for several weeks until it can be done almost anywhere, providing you with an instant relaxation tool anytime you need one. **Caution:** some people get dizzy the first few times they try roll breathing. Get up slowly and with support.

Roll Breathing with Sounds and Hand Movement

Roll breathing can be used as a deeper form of relaxation by adding hand movements and a relaxing sound to help you block out other thoughts and sounds.

"Aum" is said to be the sound of the universe. Repeating this sound can enhance the relaxed feelings you get from complete natural breathing. "Aum" is made up of three sounds — ah, ooo and mmm.

Sit in a comfortable position with your arms resting across your thighs. Inhale as you do in roll breathing, completely filling your lungs. Hold your breath for a few seconds.

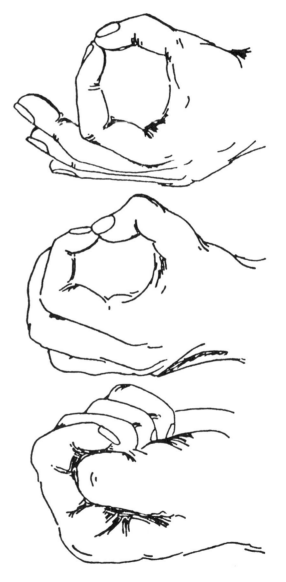

(A) As you exhale from the low chest, sound the "ah" and position your hand like this.

(B) When you exhale a third of your breath, move to the midchest and sound the "ooo." Position hands like this.

(C) Do the last third of your exhalation from your high chest. Make the "mmm" sound with your lips closed. Position your hands like this.

THE RELAXING SIGH

During the day you probably catch yourself sighing or yawning. This is generally a sign that you are not getting enough oxygen. Sighing and yawning are your body's way of remedying the situation. A sigh is often accompanied by a sense that things are not quite as they should be and a feeling of tension. A sigh releases a bit of tension and can be practiced at will as a means of relaxing.

1. Sit or stand up straight.
2. Sigh deeply, letting out a sound of deep relief as the air rushes out of your lungs.
3. Don't think about inhaling — just let the air come in naturally.
4. Repeat this procedure 8 to 12 times whenever you feel the need for it, and experience the feeling of relaxation.
5. At the end of each exhale, shake your hands away from your body as a symbol that you're throwing your tensions away.

PURIFYING BREATH

This exercise not only cleans your lungs; it also stimulates and tones up your entire breathing process and refreshes your whole body. It may be practiced by itself or combined with other breathing exercises.

1. Begin by sitting or standing up straight in good posture.
2. Inhale a complete natural breath.
3. Hold this breath for a few seconds.
4. Exhale a little of the air with a considerate force through a small hole between your lips as though you were blowing through a straw. Stop exhaling for a moment and then blow out a bit more air. Repeat this procedure until all the air is exhaled in small, forceful puffs.

PROGRESSIVE MUSCLE RELAXATION

The body responds to tense thoughts or situations with muscle tension. This muscle tension can cause pain or discomfort. Deep muscle relaxation reduces the tension in the muscles as well as general mental anxiety. You can use a pre-recorded tape to help you go through all the muscle groups or you can do it by just tensing and relaxing each muscle group. Deep muscle relaxation is effective in combatting stress-related health problems, and often helps people get to sleep.

Procedure

For best results, practice relaxation **at least once** and preferably twice daily. Choose a place which is dimly lighted and where you will be undisturbed for the period while relaxing. Pick a place which will leave your body as supported and tension-free as possible. Beds, couches, or cushions spread on the floor offer good support. Recliner chairs, large overstuffed chairs, or two chairs, one to sit on with your head resting back against the wall and the other to support your legs, are good ways for people who prefer to relax in a sitting position. If you find a good system, stay with it. If you continually fall asleep, change your positioning and/or time of day for relaxation practice.

You will find on the next pages a list of the muscle groups. Taking them in order, tense each group hard, but not to the point of cramping. Repeat any group in which you feel excessive tension. You will probably find that you have a few areas in which you experience most of your tension. These are the areas that you will want to repeat.

Tense each muscle group for 5 to 10 seconds; then give yourself 10 to 20 seconds to continue releasing and relaxing. Think about relaxing each muscle group a little more and consciously release each a little more. At various points you should go back over and review the various muscle groups and let each go a little more. Arouse yourself thoroughly by counting backwards from 5 to 1.

When practicing, you should not practice for more than about 25 minutes at a time. This should give you time enough to tense and release each muscle group once and to concentrate two or three times on those special muscle groups in which you experience tension the most. It is best not to practice the relaxation exercises twice in the same three hour period.

Muscle Groups and Exercises
1. Hands - by clenching them (then let them relax).
2. Wrists and forearms - by extending them and bending the hands back at the wrists.
3. Biceps and upper arms - by clenching your hands into fists, bending your arms at the elbows, and flexing your biceps.
4. Shoulders - by shrugging them. (Review the arms and shoulders area.)
5. Forehead - by wrinkling it into a deep frown.
6. Around the eyes and bridge of the nose - by closing the eyes as tightly as possible (contact lenses should be removed before beginning the exercise).
7. Cheeks and jaws - by grinning from ear to ear.
8. Around the mouth - by pressing the lips together tightly.
9. Back of the neck - by pressing the head back hard.
10. Front of the neck - by touching the chin on the chest. (Review the neck and head areas.)
11. Chest - by taking a deep breath and holding it, then exhaling.

12. Back - by arching it up and away from the support surfaces.

13. Stomach - by sucking it in as far as possible.

14. Stomach - by forming it into a tight knot. (Review the chest and stomach area.)

15. Hips and buttocks - by pressing the buttocks together tightly.

16. Thighs - by clenching them hard.

17. Lower legs - by pointing the feet back towards the face, like trying to bring the toes up to touch the knees.

18. Lower legs - by pointing the toes away and curling the toes downward at the same time. (Review the area from the waist down.)

With practice you will develop the skill to relax your muscles quickly and easily. Eventually you will be able to relax without the tensing part of the exercise. You will be able to do muscle relaxation using the short version below.

Short Version of Progressive Muscle Relaxation

1. Hands, forearms and biceps.

2. Head, face, throat and shoulders, including concentration on forehead, cheeks, nose, eyes, jaws, lips, tongue and neck. Considerable attention is devoted to your head area because from the emotional point of view, those muscles are the most important.

3. Chest, stomach and lower back.

4. Thighs, buttocks, calves and feet.

THE RELAXATION RESPONSE

The Relaxation Response is exactly opposite of the stress response. It returns your body to its natural balanced state as it slows the heart rate and breathing and decreases blood pressure. It helps you control your physical and mental reaction to stress. This response keeps you from using up all of your energy at once. It has been shown to be effective in helping people relieve muscle tension, reduce blood pressure, prevent stress-related health problems and sleep better.

A. Preparation

1. Quiet Environment - Find a place where there are few distractions and where you are comfortable.

2. **A Comfortable Position** - Find a position, either sitting or lying, that relieves muscular tension, yet is not so comfortable as to put you to sleep.

3. **A Mental Device** - Repeat a single syllable word like "one" silently or aloud, to break the train of distracting thoughts and to help focus your breathing.

4. **A Passive Attitude** - Adopt a let-it-happen attitude, letting thoughts come and go without worrying about how well you're performing the technique.

(Benson, Herbert, M.D., *The Relaxation Response, Avon Books, 1975*)

B. Technique - Instructions

1. Sit quietly in a comfortable position.

2. Close your eyes.

3. Begin progressive muscle relaxation — starting with your hands (tensing and relaxing) and continue until every muscle is relaxed... or if you've mastered tensing and relaxing, simply relax each muscle group. (See the description on how to do progressive muscle relaxation.)

4. Breathe through your nose — become aware of your breathing. As you breathe out say the word "one" silently or aloud. Concentrate on breathing from your abdomen, not from your chest.

5. Continue this way for 10-20 minutes, allowing thoughts to enter and exit passively.

6. Sit quietly for several minutes, until you're ready to open your eyes.

Suggestion: The technique works best if you wait until at least two hours after a meal.

BRIEF RELAXATION TECHNIQUES

These relaxation activities can be done when you need a technique and don't have very much time. They are designed to be fun and provide you with some alternatives to keep "relaxation" interesting. Schedule one of these every now and then into your regular activities. You'll be surprised at how easy it is to relax using your own imagination. Make up your own imagery after you experiment with these ideas for awhile.

1. Color Imagery

Close your eyes and scan your body for tension. Imagine the color red associated with this tension or discomfort.

Take a deep breath and change the color from red to blue and let all the tension go. Experience the relaxation associated with the color blue.

Now imagine the color blue becoming darker and darker and relax further with each shade of blue you experience.

Practice changing from red to blue with each daily hassle you confront. Imagine the color blue as your cue to relax.

2. Eye Relaxation (palming)

Put your palms directly over your closed eyes. Block out all light without putting pressure on your eyelids.

Try to see the color black. You may see other colors or images, but focus on the color black. Use a mental image to remember the color black (black fur, black object in the room).

Continue this way for 2-3 minutes thinking and focusing on black. Slowly open your eyes, gradually getting accustomed to the light. Experience the sense of relaxation in the muscles that control the opening and closing of your eyes.

3. Guided Imagery (stars and space)

Take a slow, deep breath letting your stomach rise with each inhale and fall with each exhale. Scan your body for tension and relax any area that is tense or where you're feeling any discomfort. Focus on your breathing, listening to the sound of each breath as you inhale and the whooshing sound as you breathe out.

Imagine a deep blue color of space all around you, focusing on the color blue. Imagine yourself among the stars and planets, floating suspended in a weightless blue environment.

Imagine yourself approaching a bright light. As you approach the light, observe it increasing in size. Feel yourself surrounded by the glow emanating from this light — bathed in a feeling of calmness and tranquility.

Let thoughts pass just as you imagine stars and planets passing. Let the thoughts and feelings fade into the distance. Leave them behind you.

Enjoy this time in space to relax and be comfortable — a place you can go whenever you wish. Return when you wish and remember you can go there anytime you want to feel relaxed.

Make up your own imagery, using a very peaceful place, either imaginary or real.

EXERCISE: THE NATURAL WAY TO RELAX

Exercise is the most natural way to change from stress to relaxation. Exercise can constructively use that bottled up energy and tension built up in the muscles. A long walk, a swim or a bike ride can calm anxiety, reduce depression and relax tense muscles.

For even greater calming, combine fitness activities with the breathing and mental calming techniques of this chapter. It may take some practice, but once you learn to do roll breathing while you walk, your walks will become even more refreshing and relaxing. If later you add to it the mental calming of the relaxation response, you may feel you could walk forever.

GOOD BOOKS ON STRESS

Benson, Herbert, M.D., *The Relaxation Response,* Avon Books, 1975

Davis, M., McKay, M., Eshelman, E., *The Relaxation and Stress Reduction Workbook,* New Harbinger Publications, 1980

Christensen, A., and Rankin, D., *Easy Does It Yoga for Older People,* Harper & Rowe, 1979

Pelletier, Kenneth R., *Mind As Healer, Mind As Slayer,* Delta Press, 1977

Selye, Hans, *Stress Without Distress,* J. P. Lippincott, 1974

Chapter 3
NUTRITION
Eating To Grow Younger

Introduction

As you age, three things generally happen that change both what you need to eat and what you choose to eat.

1. **Your body slows down.** The same amount of work you used to do now requires a bit less energy or food to do. Some people might see this as increased efficiency, but however you look at it, as your metabolism slows down, you need less food.

2. **Your body begins to show the effects of a long and active life.** Some or all of your natural teeth may now be replaced by dentures, food may not taste or smell quite the same as it used to, bladder control and bowel function may not be as good as they once were. As a result you may find you are eating different foods and drinking less water or other fluids.

3. **Your eating "culture" and customs change.** As you grow older, families grow up and spouses pass away. As a result, you may find that you have changed what, how often, and how much you eat. The social aspects of eating are as important as any other aspect.

So What? Do Eating Changes Really Affect Health? YES!

Your body is like a good automobile. It needs both gas and oil to keep it running smoothly. The calories in your food are like the gas. You must burn calories to make your body go. But the vitamins, minerals and fiber in your food are also essential. Like a regular oil change and "lube" job, these nutrients keep the body in balance and running smoothly.

As you age, you need less gas (fewer calories) to go where you need to go so you may eat less food. But you still need your nutrients. (Cars need more and more oil as the years go by.)

If you run out of oil, you may blow your engine. If you run out of nutrients, you may get sick. Anemia, brittle bones, hair loss, infections, thyroid problems are all related to nutrient deficiencies. Bowel cancer, constipation, hemorrhoids, and dehydration are also linked to inadequate fiber, water and nutrients.

On the positive side, eating good food will help you think clearly, have more energy and look healthy. So to prevent disease and illness, older persons may wish to improve what they eat. What is needed are more nutrient-dense foods — that is, foods that have more nutrients (oil) and fewer calories (gas) than you may be used to.

This chapter will help you to learn which eating changes might keep an older motor running smoothly.

EATING GUIDELINES AFTER SIXTY - A SUMMARY

1. Drink more water (8 glasses per day would be great).
2. Eat more starch (if this surprises you, see page 45).
3. Switch from white to whole wheat bread.
4. Don't scrimp on protein (we know some inexpensive sources).
5. Cut back on fat and sugar (much gas, little oil).
6. Reduce the amount of salt you eat (linked to high blood pressure).
7. Eat a greater variety of foods (mix your own nutrients).

Any one of these changes will increase your health and reduce your chances of illness. All of them together may enhance your over-all well-being and enjoyment of life.

WATER - THE MAGIC ELIXIR OF LIFE

The benefits of water:
1. aids in digestion
2. prevents dehydration and heat stroke
3. helps prevent constipation
4. increases blood volume — aids in circulation
5. protects throat against cold infections
6. helps to prevent and cure coughs
7. helps to prevent and cure urinary infections

Some Tips On Drinking More Water
1. Gradually increase the water you drink.
2. Drink a full glass with every meal.
3. Drink a glass when you get up in the morning (before coffee).

4. Enjoy a glass at mid-morning and mid-afternoon.

5. Limit evening water drinking so it won't disrupt your sleep.

6. Try replacing soft drinks or coffee with water.

7. To add taste, try adding a slice of lemon or orange.

8. Try drinking hot water — like tea without the tea. Some people really like it.

9. Drinking herb tea is one way to decrease caffeine intake while increasing fluid intake.

10. Drink as much water as you like. It's virtually free!

STARCH IS A GOOD GUY

How many times have you heard that starchy foods are fattening? If you have been avoiding starch as a way to lose weight — STOP and read this carefully.

1. Starches are usually packed with nutrients, vitamins and fiber.

2. Starches have less than half the calories per ounce as fats.

3. Starches are usually inexpensive.

What Are Starches?

Starchy foods like potatoes, wheat, rice, vegetables and fruits are mostly made of complex carbohydrates. Carbohydrate is the ideal fuel for most body functions. It is low in calories, high in nutrients and fiber, easily digested and comparatively low in cost.

Some people have always thought of starches as fattening. Let's look at why. A big Idaho baked potato with 2 pats of butter and 3 tablespoons of sour cream could easily contain 270 calories. That certainly could be fattening.

But how much is starch? The 3 tablespoons of sour cream account for a total of 75 calories. The 2 pats of butter amount to 90 calories, leaving just 105 calories for the basic potato — not too fattening at all.

ARE YOU EATING ENOUGH FIBER?

Fiber itself has no vitamins, nutrients or calories — yet it is an important part of what we eat.

1. Fiber aids in digesting and excreting food.

2. Fiber and fluids together prevent constipation.

3. A lack of fiber may lead to cancer of the bowels.

The "Fluffies Test"

If your bowel movements are large and soft, you probably are getting plenty of fiber. If they are small, hard and sink, you may be getting too little fiber or fluids.

A slice of whole grain bread per meal adds much needed fiber. Other delicious high fiber foods include:

- unprocessed cereals (like bran*, shredded wheat, oatmeal)
- brown rice
- popcorn
- fresh fruits and vegetables (raw or lightly steamed)

---

*Bran is not only tasty, it's also inexpensive, and can be easily added to many recipes to increase fiber content:

1. Add it to waffles, pancakes and muffins.
2. Sprinkle it on your macaroni & cheese, or tuna-rice casserole.
3. Mix it into your applesauce or scrambled eggs.

REMEMBER: When adding bran to your diet, you must increase your water intake.

PROTEIN MYTHS

There are two **misconceptions** about protein: (1) that red meat is the only good source and (2) that older people don't need much protein. Neither is true.

Fish and poultry, and even certain vegetables are excellent sources of protein. The amount of protein you need changes very little as you grow older. Protein is used by the body both for growth and for the replacement of old cells. Although older people are not growing much, the need for cell replacement increases as we age. A lack of protein can be related to anemia, fatigue, and the lack of enthusiasm for life sometimes mentioned by older persons. We know that low hemoglobin levels (the cause of most cases of anemia) can be related to the amount of protein (and iron) in a person's diet.

Although meats are good sources of protein, so are many other foods. Whole grains, dried beans, peas and nuts all contain high amounts of protein but need to be eaten in combinations to assure that all of the protein's amino acids are working.

The figure on the following page shows which non-meat foods can be put together to make a complete protein serving.

Meats would be excellent sources of protein if they didn't usually come packaged with so much fat. Even lean hamburger meat has about 20% of its calories from fat. Regular hamburger is about 30% fat.

Moderate protein consumption is recommended; too much interferes with the absorption of calcium, important to maintaining strong bones. Although loss of bone calcium is a greater problem for older women, it also affects men to a lesser degree.

PROTEIN COMBINATIONS

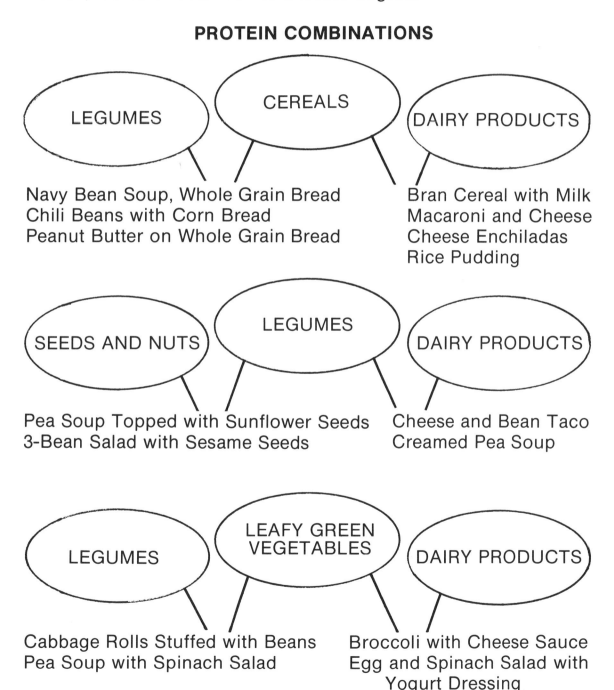

LEGUMES   CEREALS   DAIRY PRODUCTS

Navy Bean Soup, Whole Grain Bread
Chili Beans with Corn Bread
Peanut Butter on Whole Grain Bread

Bran Cereal with Milk
Macaroni and Cheese
Cheese Enchiladas
Rice Pudding

SEEDS AND NUTS   LEGUMES   DAIRY PRODUCTS

Pea Soup Topped with Sunflower Seeds
3-Bean Salad with Sesame Seeds

Cheese and Bean Taco
Creamed Pea Soup

LEGUMES   LEAFY GREEN VEGETABLES   DAIRY PRODUCTS

Cabbage Rolls Stuffed with Beans
Pea Soup with Spinach Salad

Broccoli with Cheese Sauce
Egg and Spinach Salad with
Yogurt Dressing

CHEWING THE FAT

Most people would benefit from eating less fat because it is (1) high in calories and (2) low in vitamins and minerals.

There are two kinds of fat:

1. Saturated fat (solid at room temperature) like meat fats, bacon grease, butter and shortening.
2. Unsaturated fat (liquid at room temperature) like safflower, sunflower and corn oils.

Saturated fats contain more cholesterol and may lead to heart disease. Unsaturated fats have less cholesterol but are just as high in calories and low in nutrients as saturated fat.

TO AVOID TOO MUCH FAT, SATURATED FAT, AND CHOLESTEROL

- *Choose lean meat, fish, poultry, dry beans and peas as your protein sources.*
- *Limit your use of eggs and organ meats (such as liver).*
- *Limit your intake of butter, cream, hydrogenated margarines, shortenings and coconut oil, and foods made from such products.*
- *Trim off excess fat.*
- *Broil, bake or boil rather than fry.*
- *Read labels carefully to determine both amounts and types of fat contained in foods.*
- *Use low-fat or non-fat dairy products.*
- *Watch out for hidden fats in fried foods, potato chips, nuts, and other snack foods and rich desserts.*

CHOLESTEROL AND EXERCISE

The cholesterol you eat doesn't affect your health until it reaches your blood. Cholesterol is needed to transport excess fat in the blood. The cholesterol you eat is modified by your body into two kinds of cholesterol in the blood.

Regular or low density cholesterol (LDL) acts like a fat delivery truck in the blood. It picks up fat from digestion and delivers it to the cells. When too much fat is delivered to the arteries and heart, it begins to clog them up, often causing high blood pressure and even heart attacks.

High Density Cholesterol (HDL) acts like a garbage truck. It picks up excess fat in the cells, arteries and heart, and dumps it into the bowels for excretion. Thus **HDL cholesterol protects against high blood pressure and heart disease.**

The amount of exercise people get helps to determine which kind of cholesterol winds up in the blood. The more exercise you get, the more HDL cholesterol you have. This may be one of the most important ways that exercise helps to promote health and prevent disease.

---

2 KINDS OF CHOLESTEROL

HDL - **H**igh **D**ensity **L**ipoproteins - *Removes excess fat from the body.*

LDL - **L**ow **D**ensity **L**ipoproteins - *Carries fats to all parts of the body.*

Exercise helps cholesterol work for you - not against you.

SUGAR

The average American eats 130 pounds of sugar per year. That amounts to 250,000 calories and very little else. Sugar gives you empty calories — like gas for your car but not a drop of oil or grease. You can run for a while on sugar but eventually you are going to break down.

- Sugar causes tooth decay.
- Sugar contributes to obesity.
- Sugar often takes the place of the good foods you need.

Older people with diabetes should be particularly wary of sugar.

HIDDEN SUGAR - You may be eating more than you think.
   Sugar is now added to most processed foods including breads, canned vegetables and fruits and, of course, most cereals.

Look on the label. If it contains sugar it would be listed in any of the following ways: sucrose, glucose, fructose, corn syrups, corn sweeteners, maltose, dextrose, or honey.

Be especially aware of "new" cookbooks claiming no sugar. Many times these recipes rely almost 100% on honey. There are essentially no nutritional qualities distinguishing honey from white or brown sugar.

An occasional "sweet" is not harmful. The important thing is to begin to enjoy foods without added sugars. This conditions your taste buds so that pre-sweetened foods will seem too sweet.

SOME EXAMPLES OF ADDED SUGAR IN PROCESSED FOODS

Food	Serving Size	Teaspoons Sugar In Serving	% Sugar By Calories
Coke	12 oz.	9.2	99
Hi-C Orange Drink (Welch's)	6 oz.	4.8	81
Kellogg's Corn Flakes	1 cup	.5	7
Cranberry Sauce	1/2 cup	11.7	90
Catsup	1 tbsp.	.6	61
Yogurt, Fruit	8 oz.	7.5	50
Jello, Cherry	1/2 cup	4.5	87
Beets, Pickled (Del Monte)	1/2 cup	2.1	57
Canned Peaches in Heavy Syrup	2 halves	3.5	50

TO AVOID EXCESSIVE SUGARS

1. *Use less of all sugars, including white sugar, brown sugar, raw sugar, honey, and syrup.*
2. *Eat less of foods containing these sugars, such as candy, soft drinks, ice cream, cakes, cookies.*
3. *Select fresh fruits or fruit canned without sugar or light syrup rather than heavy syrup.*
4. *Read food labels for clues on sugar content — if the names sucrose, glucose, maltose, dextrose, lactose, fructose, or syrups appear first, then there is a large amount of sugar.*
5. *Remember, how often you eat sugar is as important as how much sugar you eat.*

VARY WHAT YOU EAT DAILY

Cows can eat grass every day and stay healthy. Birds can eat birdseed day after day and do fine. A dog can get everything he needs from a single brand of dog food. But, for people, there is no single food that will sustain good health. The nutrients, vitamins and minerals our bodies need demand that we eat a variety of foods each day.

1. Vary what you eat from meal to meal and from day to day.

2. Include several foods in each meal.

3. Don't eat **too** much of any one food type. For example: eating only dairy products will not give you the iron you need; a steady diet of "fast" foods will load you up on salt.

When a person cooks and eats alone it often seems easier to prepare one thing at a time. Such a habit can rob you of certain vitamins and minerals which you need to be healthy. Always include three or more different foods in every meal.

THE 80-20 RULE

If you eat good foods 80% of the time, you don't need to worry much of the rest of the time. A slice of white bread, a donut or even a Twinkie won't hurt you if most of what you eat is wholesome, unprocessed food.

On the other hand, if most of what you eat is high fat, high sugar foods, a few "health foods" mixed in will probably not improve your health. Good eating should become a regular habit but need not exclude all less nutritious foods all of the time.

CAFFEINE IS IN MORE THAN COFFEE

While caffeine-containing and/or alcoholic beverages may not be called nutritious, they are often a part of most American diets.

Caffeine, which is found in coffee, tea, cola, chocolate and many OTC (**O**ver **T**he **C**ounter) drugs, is a central nervous system stimulant. A cup of coffee in the morning may give us a nice "pick-me-up"; however, more than one cup may cause a significant rise in pulse rate and blood pressure and makes some people feel "jumpy" or "jittery." Many people find it hard to sleep if they indulge in too much caffeine during daytime hours.

In addition to caffeine, coffee, tea and chocolate contain other substances that have much the same effect as caffeine.

WHAT'S YOUR DAILY CAFFEINE CONSUMPTION?

The three tables below list various sources of caffeine. Multiply your daily consumption with the caffeine content to find your total daily consumption of caffeine.

Coffee (fill in dose from table 1)   __ cups @ __ mg = __ mg

Tea (fill in dose from table 1)   __ cups @ __ mg = __ mg

Cola Drinks (fill in dose from table 2)   __ cups @ __ mg = __ mg

OTC (Over The Counter) Drugs (fill in dose
    from table 3)   __ tablets @ __ mg = __ mg

Other Sources (chocolate 25 mg per bar,
    cocoa 13 mg per cup)   __ cups @ __ mg = __ mg

Daily Total __ mg

I would prefer my daily total to be about __ mg

CAFFEINE TABLES

Table 1
Caffeine content of coffee, tea, and cocoa (milligrams per serving — average values).

Coffee, instant 66	Teabag - 1 minute brew .. 28
Coffee, percolated 110	Loose tea - 5 minute brew 40
Coffee, dripolated 146	Cocoa 13
Teabag - 5 minute brew .. 46	

Table 2
Caffeine content of cola beverages (milligrams per 12-ounce can).

Coca Cola 65	TAB 49
Dr. Pepper 61	Pepsi-Cola 43
Mountain Dew 55	Diet RC 33
Diet Dr. Pepper 54	Diet-Rite 32

Table 3
Caffeine content of over-the-counter drugs (per tablet).

Anacin 32	Excedrin 64
Aqua-ban 100	Midol 32
Vivarin 200	No Doz 100
Caffedine 200	Pre-mens Forte 100
Dristan 16	Vanquish 33
Empirin 32	

Source: M.L. Bunker & M. McWilliams, *Caffeine Content of Common Beverages,* Journal of the American Dietetic Assoc., Vol. 74, pgs. 28-32, January 1979

SALT

Older people should know that too much salt can contribute to high blood pressure and heart disease. Most Americans eat two to three times the salt they need. Like sugar, salt is added to most processed foods either for taste or as a preservative. If food labels contain any of the following words, chances are the product is high in salt: sodium; brine; pickled; MSG.

TO AVOID TOO MUCH SALT

- *Eat more unprocessed foods (they have less salt).*
- *Cook with only small amounts of added salt.*
- *Add salt to food at the table only if it really needs it — and then just add a little. Taste it first!*
- *Avoid salty foods, such as potato chips, pretzels, salted nuts, condiments (soy sauce, steak sauce, garlic salt), pickled foods, and cured meats.*

Recipes For Creative Salt Substitutes

1/2 tsp. cayenne pepper
1/2 tsp. garlic powder
1 tsp. each of:
  basil
  marjoram
  thyme
  parsley
  savory
  mace
  onion powder
  black pepper
  sage

Green Salad Herbs

2 1/2 T. dried parsley
2 T. chopped dried chives
1 T. thyme
1 T. basil
1 tsp. dried dill weed
1 tsp. tarragon

FISH OIL

Studies show that the omega-3 polyunsaturated oils in fish may provide significant protection against coronary artery disease. As little as one ounce of fish a day or one to two 3-5 ounce servings per week can lower your cholesterol.

ARE YOU OVERWEIGHT?

Since people come in a variety of sizes and shapes, no one weight is right for everyone of the same height and sex. The weight that is best for you depends upon your individual frame size and muscular development. It is the weight at which you look and feel your best. Some people look and feel better when they weigh somewhat more than their statistically-desirable weight, if the extra weight is largely firm muscle, not fat.

TIPS TO AVOID OVEREATING

- *Eat slowly. Try putting your fork down between each bite.*

- *Put small portions on a small plate. It will look like you're eating more than you really are.*

- *Don't turn to food when you're feeling down. It adds calories, not contentment. Try a brisk walk instead.*

- *Keep fresh fruits and veggies on hand for snacks and get the sweets out of the house.*

NUTRITION BIBLIOGRAPHY

The American Diabetic Association Family Cookbook. Prentice Hall, Inc., 1980

Ballantine, Rudolph, M.D., *Diet and Nutrition, A Holistic Approach.* The Himalayan International Institute, Honesdale, Pa., 1979

Branfen, Nan, *Nutrition for a Better Life, A Source Book for the '80's.* Capra Press, Santa Barbara, Ca., 1980

Hamilton, Eva May, and Eleanor Whitney, *Nutrition, Concepts and Controversies.* West Publishing Company, St. Paul, Mn., 1979

Middleton, Katherine, and Mary Abbott Hess, *The Art of Cooking for the Diabetic.* Contemporary Books, Inc., 1978

Medical Self Care, The Quarterly Magazine of Access to Health Tools (Food and Health issue, #14, Fall, 1981)

Nutrition and Health, Dietary Guidelines for Americans, USDA. U.S. Department of Health and Human Services, Home and Garden Bulletin #232, 1980

Robertson, Laurel, Carol Flinders and Bronwen Godfrey, *Laurel's Kitchen.* Nilgiri Press, Petaluma, Ca., 94953, 1976

Chapter 4
SELF-CARE
You and Self-Care

You are the person best qualified to keep yourself healthy and know when you are ill. You know yourself better than anyone else. With a little practice, you can learn the skills to find out what is normal for you. Best of all, you can combine your experience with some new skills and techniques to manage most minor health problems. For those problems that require the assistance of a health professional, there's still much you can do for both prevention and treatment.

You and your doctor can work together to create a health care team far more effective than either one of you working independently of the other.

This chapter will provide you with some suggestions for things you can do on your own, as well as some tips on how to work with your doctor when professional help is needed. If you learn these skills and increase your knowledge while you're feeling well, you'll be able to quickly put them to work for you at the first sign of discomfort or illness.

THE ART OF SELF-CARE

Self-Care is accepting personal responsibility for our own health. Americans already handle about 70% of their health problems without the assistance of a health professional. A little training in self-care skills and attitudes will enable us to handle those health problems more effectively and with greater confidence.

Self-Care is adopting healthy life style habits of fitness, relaxation and nutritional wellness, with support from our family and friends.

Self-Care is learning how to make the changes you choose to make to do the things you want to do. It includes keeping accurate personal health records; monitoring health measures such as temperature, pulse, blood pressure and weight; and doing your own home physical exams.

55

Principles of Self-Care*

1. Become a specialist in yourself. LISTEN TO WHAT YOUR BODY TELLS YOU.

2. Give your body the first chance at making you well.

3. Keep written records . . . let the past guide the future.

4. Treat medications with suspicion and respect. Know the benefits and side effects of every drug you take.

5. Accept no treatment you don't understand.

6. You are the chief executive of your health. Save all important decisions for yourself.

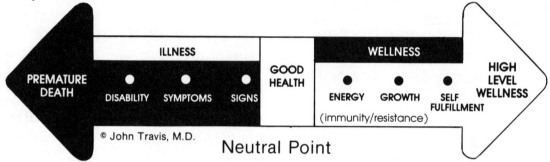

7. Health is more than the absence of disease. Self care should lead to high level wellness and GROWING YOUNGER.

8. Choose a doctor with whom you can work.

* Concept by Donald Ardell, Ph.D.

The pages that follow describe some common self-care activities that you can learn for yourself starting today.

DOING A HOME SELF-CARE EXAM

The Importance of the Home Self-Care Exam

Home examinations are one step in taking responsibility for your own health. You are the person who knows yourself best. A good home self-care exam will help you learn what's normal for you so you can recognize a problem when it arises.

This section outlines the steps in a home self-care exam. Completing the exam is fun and easy, and shouldn't take more than half an hour. **Learn the routine with a friend or family member so you can help each other with your exams.**

The home self-care exam isn't only for routine check-ups. When you become ill, complete the exam and compare the results with an exam given when you were well. Record all self-care exams on the Home Self-Care Exam form found in the last chapter, **Your Health Records,** on page 122. **You need** good clear written records, for no one can remember everything.

While periodic home self-care exams are not a substitute for a professional examination, they can provide information which will make that professional exam more worthwhile.

By knowing what's involved in a home self-care exam, you'll know better what's going on in an office physical exam. You will be better able to ask good questions and to understand what your health professional tells you.

Before the Exam

Home self-care exams will be easier if you follow the same routine each time. Do the exam in a comfortable, well-lighted room where interruptions will be limited. Exams should be pleasant experiences. Relax and have confidence. Your attitude is as important as your skills.

Tools You'll Need

Doing a good, thorough home self-care exam requires only a few tools:

- a penlight or flashlight
- an accurate thermometer
- a tongue depressor (a butter knife or the end of a spoon works well)
- a clock, stopwatch or watch with a sweep second hand
- a bathroom scale and a tape measure
- disposable gloves for rectal examination
- mirror

Your own Home Self-Care Form is found on page 122.

VITAL SIGNS

Taking the vital signs is the easiest way to measure the life sustaining functions of the body. The 3 most essential vital signs are pulse (rate of heart beat), respiration (breath rate), and the body temperature. Monitoring your blood pressure, height, and weight is also valuable.

It is important to have records of a person's vital signs when the person is well, to have a standard for comparison if illness comes.

Weight records can be useful in diagnosing an illness. Sudden weight loss or gain accompanies some illnesses. Weigh at the same time of day, undressed. Measure height without shoes.

Temperature, too, can be useful in diagnosis. Normal is 98,6° orally, but varies by individual, so it is important to determine a normal temperature for each person. Temperatures vary with time of day and other factors, so take the temperature 3 times a day, on several different days, to decide what is average.

When reference to temperature is made, it will be an oral temperature. Since rectal and oral temperatures vary only 1 degree, the difference is not critical, but you should know the kind of temperature if you need to discuss it with a health professional.

Details of how to take a temperature and measure the other vital signs are given on pages 69-71.

REASON FOR PHYSICAL

Write down why the exam is being done: person is ill, or a routine check.

MENTAL HEALTH OBSERVATIONS

Note the general outlook (anxious, cheerful, depressed, etc.), and any recent events, changes, etc., that have affected your mood or attitude.

SKIN

Look at **all** the skin for overall tone and color. Look for moles, warts, bruises, cuts, boils, lumps, rashes, birthmarks, insect bites, etc. You're becoming familiar with the skin, so the next time you do an examination, you can note any changes. The first time write down the size and location of everything you observe. In subsequent exams, note any changes. Record the condition of the skin: dry, oily, sweaty, etc.

SKULL, HAIR, SCALP

Learn what is normal. Feel the skull for lumps, bumps, or tender areas. Check the hair. When normally healthy hair looks dull, make a note of it. Look for bald spots on the scalp, flakiness, or dandruff.

EYES

Check for crustiness or flaking on eyebrows or eyelashes. Look for matter in eyes, redness in whites of eyes, or excessive tearing. Do the Pupil Constriction Test, as described on page 69.

NOSE

Check to see that the person breathes through both nostrils. Examine discharge, if any. Write down the color, and whether it is thick or thin. To better see the inside of the nose, flatten it and gently push up. Use a penlight to examine the tissues inside the nose. Note whether they are pink and healthy-looking or gray, blue, red or inflamed. Apply firm pressure on the sinuses to test for tenderness.

EARS

Check the outer ear and behind the ear for crustiness, and wiggle the outer ear to test for tenderness. Use a penlight to look in the ear canal for wax. Pull the ear lobe gently to see into the canal more clearly. Note if the wax is thin and runny, thick, brown, black, or whatever. If you are examining another person, note if there is an odor to the ear.

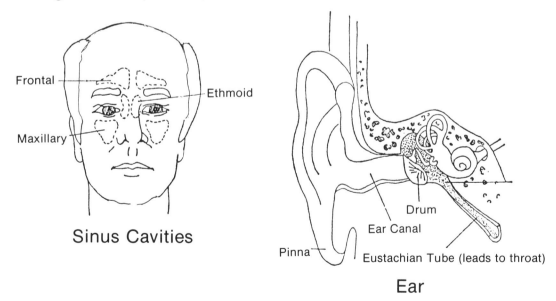

Sinus Cavities

Ear

HEARING

The following simple test is a very rough check for hearing. Any possible problem discovered with this test should be thoroughly investigated by a health professional.

59

Use a clock, watch, or some other object which makes a stable, quiet sound. Hold the clock out of sight some distance from one side of the person's head, and slowly move closer. Ask the person, or note when you hear the ticking first. Repeat for the other ear. The sound should be heard about the same distance away from each ear. A more complete explanation of the hearing test is found on page 85.

MOUTH

Using a penlight, check inside the mouth for sores or white spots on the lips, tongue, cheeks, and under the tongue. Using your finger, feel inside the mouth for growths. Most tumors that develop in the mouth are abnormal shapes, or easy to feel. Healthy gums are pink, sometimes grayish, firm and strong. They grow tightly around each tooth. Record any tenderness, puffiness or bleeding in the gums or if the seal around the base of each tooth appears to be pulling away.

Examine the teeth for black or brown spots or holes (possible cavities). Check to see if the teeth are clean or if there is obvious plaque. If natural teeth are absent, remove dentures and examine mouth and gums for areas of irritation or swelling beneath the dentures. Dentures should fit snugly and not be irritating to mouth or gums.

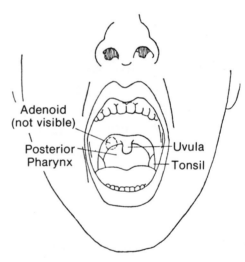

Mouth and Throat

THROAT

Have the person open the mouth as wide as possible. If necessary, push the tongue down with the end of a spoon or a butter knife to let you see way back in the throat. Using a penlight, check the back of the throat for color and appearance. Check for swollen or bright red tonsils, if they are there. While tonsils frequently atrophy and disappear between ages 40-50, they can be seen in younger persons. Healthy throat tissue is pink and moist. Note anything red, swollen, white or yellow. Notice if there is yellow or white mucus draining down the back of the throat (the pharynx).

NECK

Check the neck for swollen lymph nodes and for flexibility. The lymph system acts as a filter for infection, destroying bacteria brought to the nodes by white blood cells. Lymph nodes are located throughout the body and will swell when there is an infection in a nearby part of the body. For example, the node at the groin would swell if there were an infected cut on the thigh.

Lymph Nodes of the Neck

In the home self-care exam, you are most concerned with the lymph nodes in the neck, although you should certainly make note of any unusually swollen node.

To examine the lymph nodes in the neck, place your hand directly under the left jaw. Have the person (or yourself) relax, then tilt the head slightly to the left. Start under the chin and feel gently with the fingertips for little lumps, the lymph nodes. Work up to under the ear and then do the same for the right side. On a healthy adult, you won't feel the nodes. With a minor infection, the nodes may enlarge to the size of lima beans. History of past infections, and knowing what's normal for the person are important in this case. The neck should also be examined for any unusual lumps or bumps. A cyst is an enclosed pouch or sac of skin, often filled with mucus or oil-like material. It is not serious, but should be reported to a health professional. Also check the neck for flexibility. Ask the person to touch chin to chest, and note the ease/difficulty with which this is accomplished.

CHEST, BREAST

Look at the chest for symmetry (same on both sides) and to see how the person normally breathes — with chest or abdomen. Listen for breathing sounds, harshness, raspiness, irregularity, whistling, dry crackling, or gurgling sounds. These are signs to discuss with your health professional.

BREAST SELF-EXAM

Breast self-exam should be done monthly. Breast cancer is the number one cancer killer among women, yet, if caught early, it is highly curable. Over 95% of breast lumps are discovered by women themselves, so it is very important for each woman to take responsibility for checking her breasts monthly.

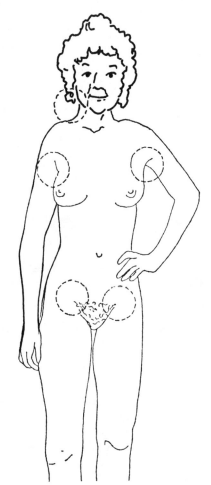

Lymph Nodes of the Body

Although breast cancer primarily affects women, it occasionally strikes men, accounting for 0.2 percent of all male cancers. It occurs more often in black men than in white men, affecting 10 black men in every million and 7 white men in every million.

Establish a regular time each month to examine your breasts. A good time for menopausal women is the first day of each month.

Begin your breast examination in the shower or bath when your hands are wet and soapy and glide easily over the skin. With your fingers flat, move gently over every part of each breast. Use your left

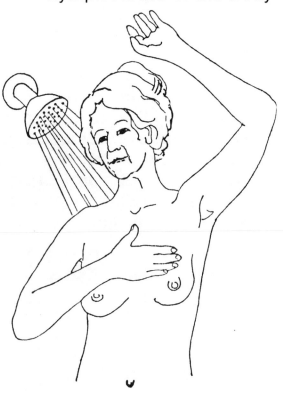

Self-Breast Examination Starts in the Shower

hand to examine the right breast. Check for lumps or thickening.

Next examine your breasts visually before a mirror. You are looking for any dimpling, puckering, retraction of the skin, or any changes in the contour of the breast. A monthly examination will help you become familiar with your body so you can recognize any changes. Next, lift the arms above the head and again inspect the breasts. Few women have left and right breasts that match exactly. Learn what is normal for you.

Now place the heels of your hands together in front of your chest and press together. Again, look for dimpling or any skin changes.

The third step of the breast examination is done lying down. Place a pillow or a folded towel under the shoulder of the side you will examine. Place your arm at your side. Feel for lumps.

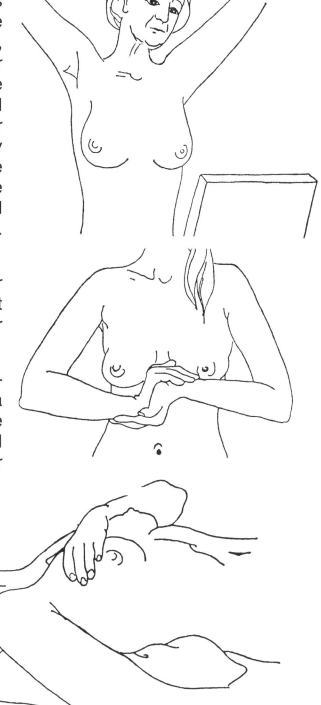

Use your right hand to examine the left breast. With fingers relaxed, use the flats of the fingers in gentle circular motions, and examine the inside of the breast. Be sure to cover all the breast tissue, with particular attention to the nipple area. Feel the area over the breastbone (sternum) also.

You are feeling for lumps, thickening, or changes of any kind. To examine the outside of the breast, place your left arm under your head. Now using the flat of your fingers, in a circular motion, examine all the tissue on the outside of the breast. Feel from your collarbone to your bottom rib and from your breastbone to the midline under your arm.

Next squeeze the nipple of the breast gently between thumb and index finger. Notice, too, if there is any kind of discharge from the nipple. Repeat this procedure for the other breast.

If you discover any lumps, thickening, or changes of any kind, you should report these to your doctor immediately. Remember, most lumps are not malignant, but only a physician can make a final diagnosis. You can get further information about breast examination from your physician or the local cancer society.

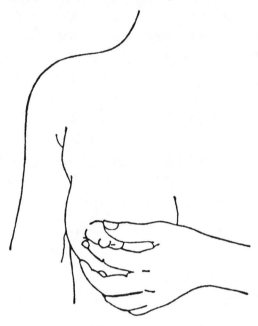
Examine Nipples

If you detect cysts in your breast, draw a diagram of your breast and mark the locations of the cysts. You will easily find them the next month to determine if they have changed or you have others.

If you start a habit of examining your breasts monthly, you'll learn what's normal and quickly recognize when something is not normal.

SPINE

Use a yardstick to measure flexibility. Hold it in your hand with the 1″ end turned toward you and touching the floor. Bend forward as far as you comfortably can, reaching both hands toward the floor. When you have reached the lowest point you can comfortably reach and hold, look at the number next to your fingertips. Record this number in your home self-care exam record. If you touched the floor, record as fingertips, knuckles, or palms.

In your home physical, you'll be checking for any obvious curvature of the spine. Curvature is often caused by poor posture.

To check the spine, have the person bend over and reach toward the floor. Place a dot of ink on each vertebra that sticks out. When the person stands up, the dots should form a straight line. If the abnormal curvature is new, report it to your health professional. If it has been present for a period of time, note any apparent increase or decrease of the curve.

ABDOMEN

To check the abdomen, divide it mentally into 4 areas or quadrants. The person should be undressed at least to the level of the pubic hair line at the pelvis. Make the person as comfortable as possible: put a pillow under the head, and keep the room comfortably warm. Have the person lie down, hands resting on chest, knees slightly bent.

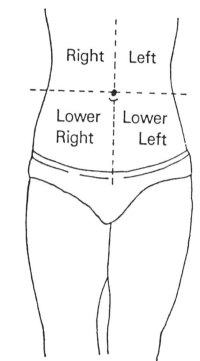

Abdominal Quadrants

Notice whether the person's abdomen is normally flat or bulged out. Feel the abdomen in all quadrants, using hands as shown. Press gently, asking if there is pain, and watching for flinching. Normally, the abdomen will be soft and you will not be able to feel any organs. Note if you do feel any masses. Also make a note of any hard or rigid surfaces. A hard smooth mass at the center of the bottom of the abdomen is probably only a full bladder. (It's a good idea to ask the person to empty their bladder before doing a physical.)

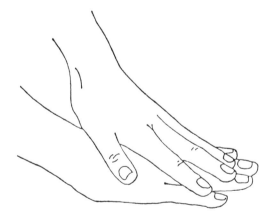

Inguinal hernias are found in the groin, most frequently in males. Hernias are sections of the intestine which bulge out between weakened sections of abdominal muscle.

To check for an inguinal hernia in males, look at the area just above the scrotum, at the groin, for any soft or bulging areas. This can be seen most easily if the person is coughing, laughing, or crying.

GENITALS

Male: The size of the penis and scrotum will vary. To examine a male's genitals, look at the penis for sores, red spots or "pimples." Now check the glans (the head of the penis covered by the foreskin in uncircumcised males) to check the urinary opening (urethra) at the tip of the glans. In uncircumcised males, do not force the foreskin back. The waxy substance under the foreskin is a normal lubricant.

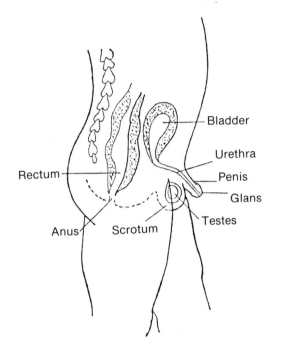

Male Genitals

Also examine the scrotum (the sac which holds the testes). Note any sores or red areas. Notice whether both testes are present in the scrotum. Apply gentle pressure. You should feel two, one in each side of the scrotum.

There should be no pain or discomfort on urination. Urine should come out in a fairly steady stream, without straining. Urine should be pale yellow and there should not be a strong odor, which may be a sign the urine is too concentrated (a clue to possible dehydration).

Strain, pain, or dribbling on urination are symptoms which may indicate an enlarged prostate, and should be discussed with a health professional. Swelling, bluish discoloration, pain, or tenderness of the scrotum will require medical attention.

Males over 40 should have an annual prostate exam by a health professional.

Female: A female's genitals are formed by the outer lips or labia majora and the inner lips or labia minora. They surround the urinary opening and the vaginal opening, and the clitoris (the front part where the two sets of lips come together).

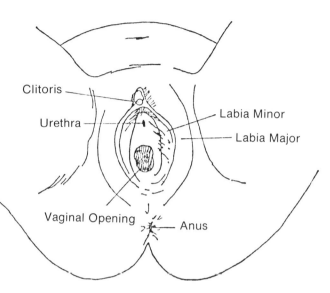

Female Genitals

Examine the entire genital area for any sores, red swollen areas, or discharge. The area inside the two lips should be pink and moist.

There should be no pain or straining on urination and the urine should come out in a fairly steady stream. The color should be pale yellow and there should be no strong odor.

Older women should have a yearly Pap smear test to detect early stages of cancer of the cervix. Cancer detected at this early stage is almost always curable. Do not douche on the day of your Pap smear. Also don't have a Pap smear if you have a vaginal infection; treat it first. Douching or infections can make the Pap test inaccurate.

ANUS

The anus is the opening where the bowel movement or stool comes out. This area is usually darker in color than the surrounding skin and is wrinkled together when closed. It stretches open for release of a bowel movement and then closes again.

Check for cuts or sores beside the anus, and for swelling. Bright blood in the stools probably indicates there are fissures (little splits or tears) in the skin of the anus, or hemorrhoids (see page 88 regarding hemorrhoids). These should be seen by a health professional.

Checking for blood in the stool can be done with a simple procedure called the hemocult test, available from your local cancer society for a small fee.

A black or tarry stool can be a sign of internal bleeding and should be brought to the immediate attention of your health professional. Be aware of any medicine you might be taking that might cause your stools to be black in color (such as iron or Pepto Bismol).

You should know the regular pattern of your bowel movements. Make a note of it on the exam record. Remember that "regular" does not mean daily for everyone. (See Constipation, page 87.)

LEGS AND ARMS

The legs and arms should each be of equal length. Check to see if one shoulder blade is higher than the other. Many people have one limb slightly shorter than the other, but it is important to know what is normal for each person.

Look for swollen joints, especially the ankles. Move the arms and legs in a full range of motion to test for flexibility. Record any stiffness or pain on movement.

HANDS AND NAILS

Examine the hands for calluses, warts, and sores. See whether both hands are about the same size and opposing fingers the same length. Nails should be clean and trimmed and not brittle, excessively thick, or peeling.

You should check for a good firm grip. Also become familiar with the size and shape of fingers so any thickening or clubbing will be recognized.

FEET AND NAILS

Check the feet for sore spots or calluses, for unusual lumps, and for unusual growths (planter's warts) on the soles of the feet. Both feet should be similar in length and toes, too, should match. When the person is standing, there should be an open space between the ball of the foot and heel — this is the arch. Usually "flat feet" (absence of arches) aren't a problem unless the person has discomfort when walking Look between the toes for any sign of infection such as athlete's foot. Check the nails for brittleness, abnormal thickness, peeling, or infection.

Move the legs and feet about to check for joint flexibility and/or pain on movement.

LUNG AND HEART SOUNDS

This exam is only possible if you have a stethoscope. Place ear pieces of the stethoscope into the ears, pointing forward, toward the eardrum. Place the stethoscope on the person's back. Listen all over the back above the waistline to the right and left of the spine. You are listening to learn what normal breathing sounds are for that person, so you can recognize when there is a change from normal. Ask the person to take a deep breath through the mouth and exhale slowly.

Repeat this process, with the stethoscope on the chest. If the person is a hairy-chested male, you will hear the hairs scratch against the stethoscope. With a fleshy or heavily muscled person, you may not be able to hear the breath sounds.

Next, listen for the heartbeat. Place the stethoscope near the nipple about 3 inches left of the middle of the chest. Count the heartbeats, which are the same as the pulse.

PUPIL CONSTRICTION TEST
(Using Penlight)

This test is used to determine how the pupils, or dark centers of our eyes, ordinarily constrict (get smaller) and how they appear after a head injury. (Usually one or both will not constrict when there is a severe head injury.)

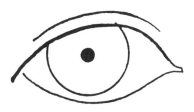

"constricted"

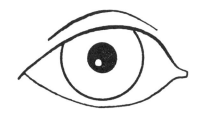

"normal"

Checking Normals:
In a darkened room use a penlight to direct light from the right side into the right pupil. Watch the pupil constrict (get smaller). It does this to cut down the light reaching the eye. Do the same for the left side. Pupils should constrict to about the same size, at about the same rate. Some people normally have different sized pupils. It is important for you to know what is normal for you. Study your own pupils in a mirror to determine your own "normal."

HOW TO TAKE A TEMPERATURE

A fever is body temperature that is raised abnormally. An active person on a hot day may have a temperature of 100° Fahrenheit (F.) without being ill at all.

If there is an acceptable reason for a slightly higher temperature (hot day, minor cold) and the person otherwise seems okay, there is no cause for concern. Smoking, drinking, or eating should be avoided for one-half hour prior to taking an oral temperature because they will cause a change in the temperature inside the mouth and lead to a false reading.

Normal temperature can range from 97.6° to 99.6° orally. Fever occurs when the body is trying to fight off an infection. A higher body temperature helps the body fight off infection, but too high a fever can be harmful. There is no medical need to reduce a temperature until it is over 102° orally, but you may wish to reduce the fever if the person is uncomfortable. Occasionally an older person can feel rather ill and not have any temperature elevation at all, so don't use temperature as your only guideline to assessing health or illness status.

The person with a fever needs to drink extra water, as fever burns off body liquids faster than normal.

Procedure for Taking an Oral Temperature

Although you can take a temperature three different ways — orally, rectally or axillary (under the armpit), an oral temperature is probably the simplest and most accurate way.

- Wash off the bulb, where the mercury is, and the lower part of the thermometer with cool, soapy water (hot water may break the thermometer). Hold the thermometer tightly by the end opposite the bulb and "shake it down," as if you were trying to shake drops of water off the bulb. This is needed to lower the mercury below 95° on the thermometer. Since the thermometer can easily slip from your hand, shake it over a bed or soft object.

- In taking the oral temperature, be sure the lips are closed and the thermometer is under the tongue. Have the person breathe through the nose. This may be more difficult with a stuffy nose. Keep the thermometer in place for 3 minutes.

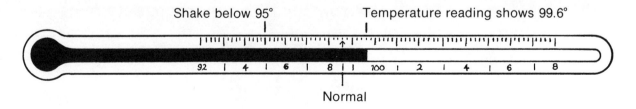

Reading a Thermometer

70

READING A THERMOMETER

Note that the thermometer is graduated from 92 degrees to 108 degrees. Each large mark indicates 1 degree of temperature. Between large marks are 4 small marks. Each small mark stands for 0.2 degrees (two-tenths of a degree).

Read the thermometer in good light. Holding the end opposite the mercury bulb, rotate the thermometer slowly until you can see a silver (sometimes red) ribbon of mercury. The place where the ribbon stops indicates the temperature reading. Write it down, noting the time of day.

HOW TO MEASURE BREATHING RATE (RESPIRATION)

Respiratory rate is how many breaths a person takes in a minute. The best time to count respiration is when the person is resting, perhaps after taking the pulse. If you keep your fingers on the pulse the person won't be aware you are counting breaths. This will give you the most accurate count. The person's breathing is apt to change if he/she sees you count the rate

Count the rise and fall of the chest for one full minute, or for 15 seconds and multiply by 4. Also notice whether there is any "sucking in" beneath the ribs or other abnormality.

Record the respiration rate.

As a person's temperature rises, the respiration rate will increase.

> *Normal resting respiration rate for those 60 and older is 15-20 breaths per minute.*

YOU AND YOUR BLOOD PRESSURE

Your blood pressure is measured by two numbers #1 / #2 :

> #1 is the pressure in your arteries as the heart contracts (called systolic pressure).

> #2 is the pressure between beats when your heart is relaxed (diastolic).

Because high blood pressure (or hypertension) may damage your heart and blood vessels by making them work harder, your job is to keep your blood pressure down.

Your goal should be to keep your diastolic (#2) pressure under 95 (under 85 would be better). The systolic pressure (#1) is not quite as important.

SOME FACTS ABOUT HIGH BLOOD PRESSURE

1. One in every six adult Americans has it to some degree.
2. You may have it and not know it.
3. Hypertension is not the same as nervous tension.
4. If you have it, you can control it.
5. In most cases, high blood pressure is a lifelong condition.

WHAT CAUSES IT

While the cause of high blood pressure is not completely understood, we do know that it is definitely affected by:

1. Prolonged frustration or stress
2. Heredity, or family tendencies
3. Excessive salt, fat and/or calories in your diet
4. Age. High blood pressure is more frequent in men than in women up to age 55, but the reverse is true after age 55.
5. Low level of fitness; not enough activity and exercise.
6. Smoking

WHAT ARE THE SYMPTOMS OF HIGH BLOOD PRESSURE?

- **The first symptom may be sudden death.**
  High blood pressure often has no prior symptoms. That's why a regular blood pressure check is so important.

- **Sometimes** the following symptoms can be warning signs:
  - Shortness of breath
  - Nosebleeds
  - Headaches
  - Dizziness

  These are usually present only when high blood pressure becomes very severe.

What You Can Do to Lower Your Blood Pressure

- *Lose weight.*
- *Cut back on salt.*
- *Cut back on fat.*
- *Increase your fitness activities.*
- *Learn to relax.*
- *Learn to take your own blood pressure.*
- *Get medical help if your efforts aren't successful.*

Learn to Measure Your Blood Pressure

If you have high blood pressure, the purchase of a blood pressure cuff and a stethoscope may be a good investment. Have your family or a friend who knows how to take blood pressure check frequently. Know what your blood pressure is and what it should be. Keeping a record of your blood pressure will help you determine if your efforts to keep it down are really working.

Lose Weight

Weight reduction decreases the workload on your heart and makes you look better and feel better, too. Every pound of fat adds five miles of blood vessels that your heart has to push blood through. By losing weight you lighten the load. (See Chapter 3, Nutrition, page 43.)

Eat Less Salt

Even a moderate reduction in salt may lower your blood pressure. On the average, Americans consume three times the salt we need. To learn how you might cut back on salt see Chapter 3, Nutrition, page 53.

Eat Less Fat

Fats, particularly cholesterol, seem to clog arteries and increase blood pressure. (See Chapter 3, Nutrition, page 48.)

Exercise for Health

Regular aerobic exercise will gradually lower your blood pressure while strengthening your heart. It's a great way to relax the mind while toning up the body!

Relax More

Deep muscle relaxation, meditation, and roll breathing can lower your blood pressure by helping you to relax. (See Chapter 2, Stress, pages 27-41.)

HOW TO TAKE A BLOOD PRESSURE

You'll need a blood pressure cuff (sphygmomanometer) and a stethoscope, available at most drug stores.

Procedure:

What follows is a description of the steps for taking blood pressure. While the procedure is a relatively simple one, it is recommended that you attend a brief course in taking blood pressures, often available through your local Red Cross or Emergency Medical Service, in order to assure accurate readings.

1. Sit beside a table, with a bare arm outstretched. Rest the arm on the table for support and comfort. Loosen the valve by turning it counter-clockwise and deflate the cuff completely.

2. Wrap the blood pressure cuff snugly around the arm with the lower edge of the cuff one inch above the crease at the elbow. Be sure the tubing going to the gauge is closest to the body and the tubing going to the bulb is away from the body.

3. Close the valve of the bulb and pump the bulb to raise pressure to a level of about 160 on the gauge. If you hear a heartbeat right away, then pump it up higher until you no longer hear a heartbeat. Immediately loosen the valve a bit so the needle starts moving down slowly. Don't leave the cuff pumped up; the pressure is uncomfortable.

Blood Pressure Cuff

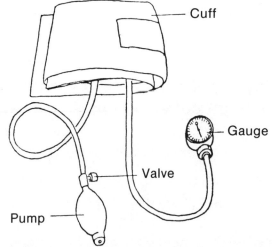

4. Watch the dial as you listen with the stethoscope. You will soon hear a tapping sound — this is the pulse sound. The number on the dial when you first hear the pulse sound is the **systolic pressure.** A typical systolic pressure might be 125.

5. As air continues to escape from the cuff, the sound will eventually disappear completely. Note where the needle is when the sounds disappear. This is the **diastolic pressure.** A normal example would be 70.

6. Open the valve completely, let the pressure fall to zero, and remove the cuff.

7. Record the reading, systolic/diastolic (125/70 for the above example).

Always repeat the procedure to be certain of your measurements. If you need to recheck your measurement, be sure the cuff is entirely deflated before inflating it again. Otherwise, your new measurement will be inaccurate. If you cannot get a clear reading after two tries, use the other arm, or wait five full minutes. You should always take a blood pressure twice to be certain of your reading.

An adult has a normal blood pressure of under 140/90. Anything over that should be remeasured and then reported to a health professional.

Taking a blood pressure reading correctly is not difficult but requires practice. You should review the procedure with your health professional.

Medications for High Blood Pressure

Sometimes medications are used to reduce high blood pressure. If this is the case, be sure you know about the medication you are taking; name, strength, dosage, and how it may affect you in addition to lowering your blood pressure. Don't stop taking it just because you feel good. Work with your health care professional in adjusting dosages and dealing with side effects.

Write down everything about your high blood pressure medications (See pages 93-98).

MY HEALTHY BACK

Back problems, especially pains in the lower back, are one of the most common health problems of men and women at any age (half of us get back pain at some time or other). Back problems can be caused by physical or emotional stress.

Your back bears the weight of the top half of the body, and transfers it to the pelvis, the seat or the feet. The soft discs between the vertebrae help support the weight and the spine has a series of curves to allow for better shock absorption and flexibility. Thirty-one pairs of nerves radiate out from the spinal cord inside the backbone. Taking good care of this equipment is of great importance.

BACK CARE

If you become less active as you grow older, back problems may become more apparent. Inactivity weakens your back and abdominal muscles which are essential to a healthy back. Maintaining good posture, with the correct degree of curve (lordosis) as illustrated, is good backache prevention.

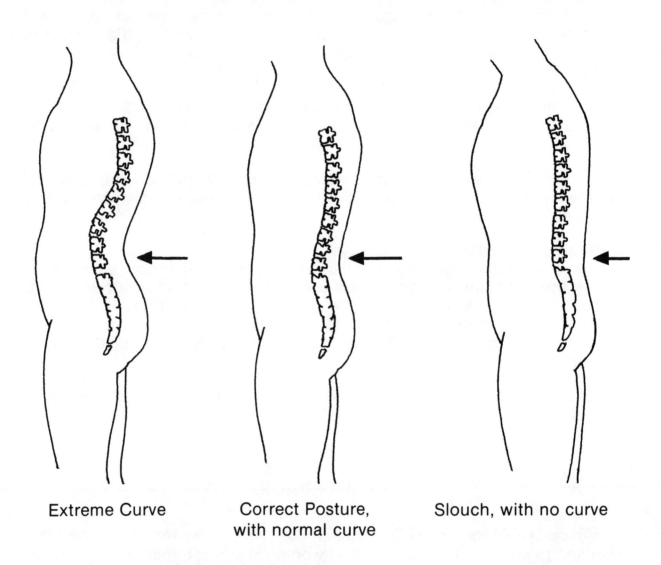

Extreme Curve   Correct Posture,   Slouch, with no curve
                             with normal curve

Pain and tension in the back are common problems. The causes may vary, from overstretching and improper positions in lifting or standing, to incorrect posture. Exercises to keep the right degree of curve in the lower back, increase flexibility, and strengthen the back and abdominal muscles, as well as correct posture, are helpful in preventing backaches.

Establishing the Right Curve for Your Back

Sit on a stool of chair height, or sit sideways on a kitchen chair. Slouch completely with your back in this position (a), relaxing for 2-3 seconds.

Then with a smooth motion draw yourself up to arch backward, making the curve extreme. Hold this position (b), for about **5 seconds**. Then return to the slouched position, with a gently rocking motion. Repeat this exercise 3-5 times, 4 or 5 times a day. There may be some feeling of strain in the extreme curved (lordosis) position but it should wear off in a few days.

Your **correct sitting position** is found by taking the extreme curved position and then releasing about **10%** of this extreme, to this position (c).

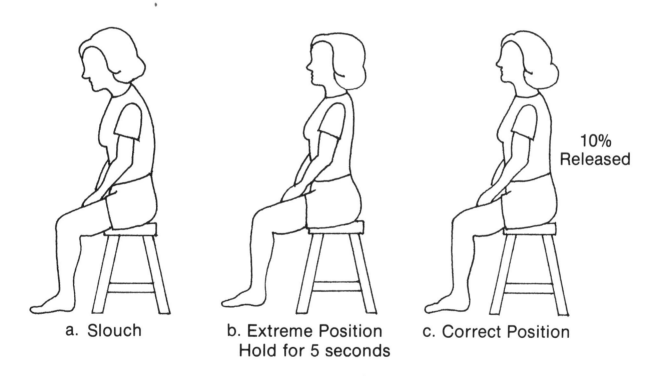

a. Slouch

b. Extreme Position
   Hold for 5 seconds

c. Correct Position

10%
Released

If your chairs do not help you maintain this degree of curve in your low back, a rolled towel or small, bolster-shaped pillow will help.

Practice the following six exercises to avoid many back problems.

1. To Decrease Tension in Back

Lie on your back with knees bent and feet shoulder width apart, rock your knees gently from side to side until you feel the tension in your back decrease.

2. To Relieve Stiff, Sore Back, Increase Flexibility

In same position as preceding exercise, pull one knee at a time toward your chest. Then, keeping knees apart, pull both knees up toward shoulders. Head and shoulders should remain on the floor. Start with 3-5 repetitions, working up to 10-12. Use a gentle pull.

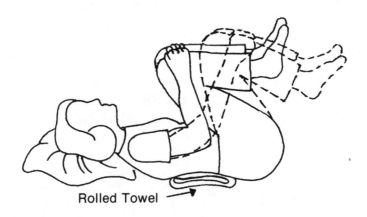

Rolled Towel

Knee-chest Exercise

3. To Strengthen and Relax Back Muscles

Lie on your back with your knees bent. Slowly lift your buttocks and then lower them. Don't hold your breath while exercising. Repeat 5 times.

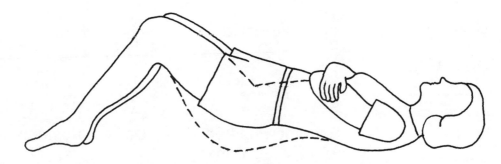

Buttocks Lift (Bridging Exercise)

4. To Strengthen Abdominal Muscles (Modified Sit-up)

Lie on your back with knees bent and arms crossed (hand to opposite shoulder). Curl your body up until your head and shoulders are about 4 inches off floor. Breathe out as you curl up and breathe in as you curl down. Repeat 5 times. Use smooth motions, not jerking the body up. **Do not** anchor your feet or straighten your knees.

5. To Increase Motion in Back

Lie on your stomach: place both arms as though to do a pushup. Slowly lift only the top part of your body as far as is comfortable. Breathe in as you roll up and breathe out as you roll down. Repeat 4-6 times.

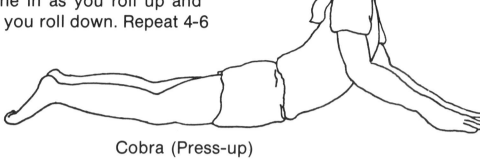

Cobra (Press-up)

6. To Relieve Low Back Tension

Lie on stomach with small pillow under your stomach. Gently rock your hips from side to side until the low back muscles feel warm and less tense. Progress to doing the exercise without the pillow. Repeat at other times during the day.

Posture

The nicest thing you can do for your back is to sit, stand, lift and sleep in positions that do not cause tension or fatigue. Stand "tall" with head up and shoulders back. If you are standing straight, a plumb line from your shoulder would pass through your hip joint, your knee joint, and slightly in front of your ankle joint.

Prolonged standing may give you low back discomfort because your back is in an extreme curved position. The discomfort may be relieved by standing tall, lifting the chest up, pulling in the abdominal muscles and tightening the buttock muscles. This reduces the extreme curve in the back.

Sitting

Sit with both feet resting on the floor, and most of your weight on your buttocks so that your hand could be easily inserted between your thigh and the front of the chair seat.

If you have been working in a stooped position with your back rounded out, stand up and gently bend backward and forward a few times. Briefly walking around helps relieve back and shoulder tension.

Sleeping

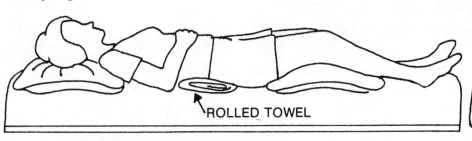

ROLLED TOWEL

A good sleeping position is on your back or side, with knees bent to a position of comfort. Use pillows at the small of your back and under your knees.

Lifting

Remember to eliminate the hollow in the back at all times, even when lifting a very small object.

1. Always lift from a squatting position, with at least one foot flat on the floor.

2. Keep your head up. If a pen falls from your breast pocket while you are lifting, you are lifting incorrectly.

3. Never lift a heavy load above the waist.

4. Avoid twisting your body while lifting, carrying or setting down a load.

ROLLED TOWEL

CURVE IN BACK

SEAT CLOSE TO STEERING WHEEL

Driving

The key to comfortable driving is keeping the knees higher than the hips. **Getting into the Car:** 1. Sit on the edge of the seat. 2. Using good pelvic tilt, slide right leg to corner of seat and then 3. bring left leg to the right leg. 4. Pivot on buttocks and slide legs under the wheel. 5. Move seat forward. 6. If seat is too low, use a pillow.

> *Hiking, biking, swimming and walking are other activities that keep the body's muscles in good tone and all are good preventive exercises for a healthy back.*

TREATMENT OF BACK PAIN

When you get a backache, try to determine the cause. If the pain seems to be mostly due to tension, poor posture, or during back-tiring activities, a warm, relaxing bath and gentle massaging can help eliminate the pain.

Back Resting Position

ROLLED TOWEL

Elevating your feet on a chair with your knees bent while lying on your back is very relaxing and is a good way to rest a tired back. A rolled towel or small pillow at small of back can give relief.

During the First 24-48 Hours:

1. Do back-rocking and knee-chest exercises (#1 & #2) every few hours.

2. Use **cold** packs for the first 24 hours.

3. Rest on back with knees propped.

4. Should pain relievers become necessary, use the **minimum.**

5. Practice the Relaxation Response to relieve tension (page 38).

After 48 Hours:

1. Continue back rocking and knee-chest exercises. (#1 & #2)

2. Gradually add the rest of the back exercises on pages 78 & 79. (#3, 4, 5 & 6)

3. Substitute **warm** baths and heating pads for cold packs.

4. Continue resting back until symptoms subside.

Low back pain sufferers often will want to see a health professional during acute episodes of back pain. Unfortunately, there is little a physician or a chiropractor can do. Muscle relaxants are sometimes prescribed to eliminate the muscle spasm pain. However, ice and proper muscle relaxation positions can usually do an equally effective job. If muscle relaxants are used, care should be taken not to reinjure the unprotected parts of the back. Since the trip to and from a health professional's office can be very painful and even harmful to your back, carefully consider the merits of home treatment first.

When to Call a Health Professional:

1. When severe back pain results from an accident or blow to the back. DO NOT MOVE AN ACCIDENT VICTIM WHO MAY HAVE AN INJURED SPINE.

2. When severe disabling pain suddenly occurs in the leg and foot **without** significant cause.

3. If substantial relief for a sprain, strain, or disc injury is not obtained within 5 days of recommended treatment at home.

4. Pain in the back is not always due to problems of the muscles and bones of the back. Abdominal or pelvic disorders may also cause back pain. Back pain from such disorders may foretell a serious condition.

I ONLY HAVE EYES FOR ME

Have your arms become too short to hold the newspaper? This is often how farsightedness (presbyopia) is first noticed. Headaches or tiredness following reading or detail work may be another sign. Reading glasses or bifocals may be useful for dealing with this eye problem which is so common among older people.

Think of the eye as your built-in camera. It requires something to see, some light by which to see it, equipment (eyeball) in good working order, and film (your brain) upon which to record the message.

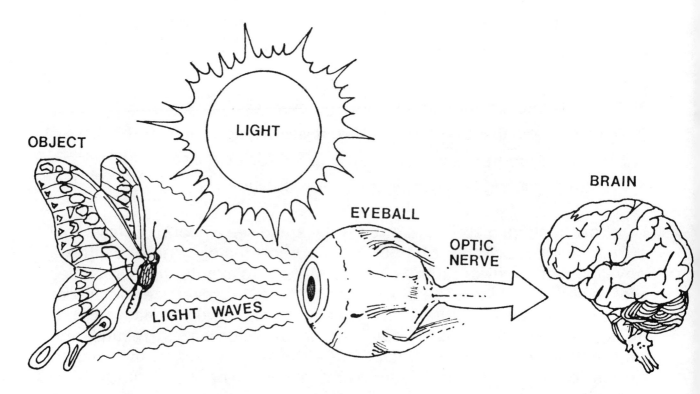

OBJECT

LIGHT

LIGHT WAVES

EYEBALL

OPTIC NERVE

BRAIN

Vision problems can be caused by changes occurring in any part of the eye. **Farsightedness,** for example, is caused by a loss of elasticity in the lens of the eye.

A **cataract** occurs when the usually clear lens gradually becomes grayish or milky colored. A cataract may first be noticed when objects seem a little "fuzzy" or seem to have halos of light around them. Looking in the mirror, the pupil in the center of the eye will be cloudy. It is usually black.

The cause of cataracts is unknown, although injury to or surgery performed on the eye may increase the risk of cataract development. The only currently known treatment is surgery, which is performed when the cataract has progressed to the point where reading, driving, or other important vision functions become difficult or impossible. This surgery, done under a local anesthesia, is usually safe, uncomplicated, and successful. A cataract operation consists of removing the clouded lens and replacing it with an implanted lens, contact lenses or special eye glasses. Each of these types of lenses has advantages and disadvantages and needs to be discussed with your physician.

Glaucoma is another major eye problem associated with aging. Glaucoma causes the blocking of the tiny passage tube for fluid, resulting in an abnormally high pressure inside the eye. This may cause tired eyes, blurred vision, one-sided headaches, or loss of peripheral (side) vision, referred to as open angle glaucoma. People who develop open angle glaucoma, the most common kind, may not be aware of any symptoms or changes until a great deal of vision has been lost.

Blindness due to glaucoma can usually be prevented through early detection. Tests for glaucoma should be taken at least once every two years by persons over age 35. Because tendencies toward developing glaucoma tend to be inherited, persons with a family history of glaucoma should have a glaucoma test every year. If glaucoma is discovered, special eye drops may be given to prevent the condition from worsening. This is important, because once vision has been lost through glaucoma it cannot be restored.

Tears help protect your eyes and keep them comfortable by keeping their delicate surface moist and by washing away irritating substances. With aging, most people manufacture fewer tears, resulting in "dry eyes" which irritate the cornea. "Dry eyes" may lead to the excessive production of watery tears which lack the proper chemical balance to soothe the eyes. To treat dry eyes, your doctor may prescribe special eye drops, called "artificial tears", or a special lubricating ointment to be used at bedtime.

Blurry vision may be caused by diseases such as high blood pressure, diabetes, hardening of the arteries, cataracts, or glaucoma, or by certain medications — such as insulin, valium, corticosteroids, and high blood pressure pills.

Eyestrain may result from reading, sewing, or other detail work, if done for long periods of time without resting or under poor light conditions.

EYE EXERCISES

There are some things that you can do for yourself to help your eyes. These exercises can be helpful in preserving your side or peripheral vision and in keeping your eyes moist and relaxed. They can help to relieve eyestrain if done on a daily basis.

1. Sit in a comfortable position. Take a deep breath and relax. Close your eyes. Think about your eyes and eyelids becoming very relaxed. Stretch your arms and shoulders gently and do a couple of slow, gentle head circles to relax your neck. Feel your eyes grow moist. Blink slowly three times and feel your eyelids carry moisturizing tears over your eyes.

2. Keeping your head still and relaxed, slowly open your eyes. Without moving your head and without straining your eyes, look slowly as far as you can to the right. Notice how much you can see. Now very slowly look back in front of you and then all the way to your left. Do this exercise two more times, then close your eyes and relax.

3. Keeping your head still and relaxed, open your eyes and slowly look up to the ceiling and down to the floor. Repeat three times, then close your eyes again and relax them.

4. Keeping your head still and relaxed, open your eyes and slowly look all the way from your upper right to way down at your lower left, then up to the right again. Repeat three times, then reverse and repeat, going from the upper left to the lower right and back once more. Close and relax your eyes.

5. Finally, look out your window and see the sky. Feel your eyes relaxing. Blink whenever you feel like it. Slowly look toward something far away, then at something close up, then at yourself. Look again at the sky, then close your eyes and relax. Your eyes will love you.

A FAIR HEARING

It is not uncommon for many people to develop some minor hearing loss as they grow older. Often soft or high pitched sounds become muted and loud sounds become annoying.

For the most part, hearing loss is caused by exposure to unhealthy noise levels, such as factory or city noises over a long period of time. Some other causes are ear infections or injury to the ear itself.

Usually, hearing loss happens gradually over a long period of time, so you may not even be aware of it.

Home Hearing Tests

To check your hearing, you can perform a simple test with the help of a friend. This test will give you only a rough idea of your hearing level. (Also see page 59 in this chapter.)

Use a clock, watch, or some other object which makes a stable, quiet sound. Your friend should hold the clock out of sight some distance from one side of your head and slowly move closer. Tell your friend when the ticking is first heard. Repeat for the other ear. You should hear the sound at about the same distance away from each ear. If you can't, or if when you test your friend's hearing, he can hear the noise from much further away than you can, continue on to the second test.

The second home hearing test is to look in the ear canal for possible wax buildup. Hearing loss may be entirely or partially due to accumulation of earwax.

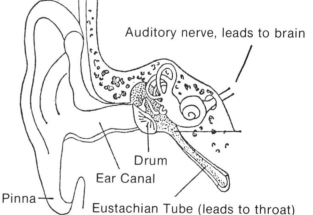

Earwax is a substance normally secreted by the ear canal to protect the ear from infection or foreign bodies. It usually dries and comes out of the ear on its own. Some people have a tendency to over-produce or accumulate earwax.

Auditory nerve, leads to brain

Drum
Ear Canal
Pinna
Eustachian Tube (leads to throat)

A feeling of "fullness" or ringing in your ears may be a symptom of accumulated earwax. To check for earwax, pull your friend's earlobe up and out and use your penlight to look into the ear canal. If the problem is wax, you will see a yellow-brown to black-colored substance blocking the ear canal. It may be sticky and soft or hard.

To prevent earwax accumulation, direct the shower spray into your ears as you bathe to keep earwax soft and prevent buildup.

To remove excess earwax, you can rinse out the ear with warm water. (Do not use this method if your eardrum is perforated.) You will need an inexpensive ear syringe available from your local pharmacy. To rinse the ear:

Fill the syringe with warm water.

Lean over the sink.

Gently squeeze the syringe and fill the ear with warm water.

Continue to fill the ear with water, allowing it to overflow into the sink.

Repeat this procedure 3-4 times a day for 3-4 days.

If you are unable to remove the excess wax yourself, consult your health professional.

If after performing these two checks you think you have a hearing problem, make an appointment with your health professional or a hearing specialist for a hearing evaluation.

Tips to Help You Hear Better

- Avoid outdoor conversations where background noise is high.
- Watch the face, especially the lips, of the person you are listening to.
- Ask the phone company for a "volume control hand set" which can more than double the sound volume of your phone. The cost in most areas is very low.
- Consider buying a hearing aid. Modern ones fit in the ear, have no wires, and are hardly noticeable. See Guidelines for Hearing Aid Users on the next page.

Tips to Help Others Hear You

- Don't shout, but speak in a slightly deeper voice.
- Look at the person you speak to.
- Use gestures and expressions freely.

If hearing loss is not recognized, it can be very disruptive to your normal life style. Don't take your hearing for granted.

Prevent ear problems by taking good care of your ears:

1. Avoid loud noise levels or wear ear plugs.
2. Keep your ears covered outdoors on cold days.
3. Keep your ears clean and check periodically for wax buildup.
4. Do **not** use small or sharp objects for cleaning your ears. This may cause damage to the ear canal or drum, and may force

wax back into the ear. To be safe, never put anything smaller than your **elbow** into your ear.

GUIDELINES FOR HEARING AID USERS

- *Make your purchase from a reputable dealer.*
- *If you are concerned about the reliability of a dealer, call the Better Business Bureau or your local Senior Citizen Center.*
- *Become an expert in the hearing aid you have chosen.*
- *Get used to wearing it gradually. Start by wearing it for a few hours and build up gradually.*
- *Be sure you remove your hearing aid before bathing or going to bed.*
- *Keep in mind that your hearing aid is designed to make voices and sounds louder but not necessarily clearer.*
- *Avoid problems by making certain the batteries are properly inserted and changed as often as necessary.*

CONSTIPATION

Constipation is the passage of hard, dry stools. If you pass soft stools, you are not constipated regardless of how "regularly" or "irregularly" you may pass them. The need for a bowel movement every day is a misconception. Some people pass stools every 3-5 days. As long as the stools are soft, such frequencies do not indicate constipation.

One of the chief causes of constipation is lack of time. The person who has had trouble with constipation should set aside a time each day, or as frequently as is normally needed, to go to the bathroom. Your bowels send you signals when there is a need to pass a movement. However, if you don't take time to heed the signal, after a while the urge will pass. Since the large intestine draws water from the stool, the stools will eventually become dry and difficult to pass.

While slowing of bowel activity may be experienced by some older people, many people retain an unchanging bowel pattern throughout their lives. In fact, older people who maintain an adequate diet, drink plenty of water, and lead active lives seldom experience difficulties with constipation.

Prevention

Diet is very important in constipation. Too few fruits, juices and clear liquids can create the problem. Susceptible people should increase the fiber in their diets by eating more bran cereals, apples and celery, and increase their water intake. (See page 45.) Regular exercise may also help prevent constipation.

Home Treatment

- Set aside relaxed times for bowel movements.
- Add juice, fruits, fiber, and water to the diet.
- Drink 2-4 **extra** glasses of water per day, especially in the morning.
- Avoid laxatives if possible. If necessary, use a stool softener or a very mild laxative. Do not use mineral oil or any other laxative regularly. Mineral oil slows the body's absorption of vitamins.

When To Call A Health Professional

- If constipation persists after the above treatment is followed for one week for adults.
- If dark blood is seen in stools. Small amounts of bright blood are usually caused by slight tearing as the stool is pushed through the anus and should stop when the constipation is controlled. More than a few streaks of bright blood should be discussed with a health professional.
- If constipation and major changes in bowel movement patterns occur and persist without apparent reason.

DEALING WITH HEMORRHOIDS

Did you know that a hemorrhoid is actually a varicose vein? While varicose veins are never nice, having them appear in such a delicate location as the rectal opening can be most unpleasant.

Hemorrhoids are veins in the rectum which become dilated and inflamed. Estimates tell us that half the people over age 50 have them. They are the most common cause of rectal problems and are aggravated by constipation, age, and prolonged standing or sitting.

Hemorrhoids can be internal (inside the anal opening) or external (protruding around the opening). They may look like small purple "lumps" around the anus.

If you don't have hemorrhoids, a diet high in fiber and water and a regular exercise program can help to keep you from getting them. If you do have them, the same things can keep your hemorrhoids under control.

Treatment for hemorrhoids may vary according to each person's own experience. Continuing your high fiber and water diet is important to soften the stool and prevent constipation. Sitting in a warm tub several times a day can be soothing, relieves itching and burning, and promotes healing. Many people find cool compresses of witch hazel and cotton balls applied to the anal area after each bowel movement is very soothing. Others swear by Vaseline as a lubricant used to ease a bowel movement. Be sure to keep the area clean and dry.

There are many hemorrhoid preparations on the market. They help to lubricate the anal area and ease both discomfort and stool passage, but generally have not been proven to be effective in reducing the swelling of hemorrhoids. For many people, Vaseline seems to work just as well.

To avoid infection, apply ointments or cream only after the anal area has been cleansed and dried.

Preparations with "caine" (Benzocaine, Nupercaine, Tetracaine, etc.) in their name or ingredients may actually increase anal irritation with repeated use.

If severe symptoms exist for more than a week, see your health professional. If a clot has formed, the vein can be lanced and the clot removed in the doctor's office.

TREATMENT FOR A HEMORRHOID ATTACK

1. *Plenty of fluids and fiber.*
2. *Warm tub baths several times each day.*
3. *K-Y Jelly or other lubricant to ease bowel movement.*
4. *Cool compresses of witch hazel and cotton balls for use after bowel movements.*
5. *Call your health professional if symptoms are:*
   - *Severe and last more than seven days.*
   - *If blood is mixed into the stool rather than on the outside.*

ARTHRITIS

Arthritis is a real pain. When it strikes, it can take the pleasure out of just about anything that you want to do. Arthritis is actually a whole group of diseases that affects the joints.

If you don't have arthritis, the best way to keep from getting it is to exercise your joints to keep them strong and flexible.

If you do have arthritis, the treatment is pretty much the same. That's right — exercise is **good** for arthritis as long as you don't overdo it. A regular exercise program with lots of joint flexing activities will keep your joints movable and your muscles strong. It is very important in preventing or reducing stiffness and weakness. (See Chapter 1 for some good joint flexing or "range of motion" exercises.)

Aerobic or endurance exercises are also important for strengthening your heart, lungs and muscles. Persons with arthritis should avoid aerobic activities that strain the joints, such as running or jogging, and stay with smooth motion exercises such as swimming or walking.

Start out slow and easy. Move the joint as far as it will comfortably go, then coax it just a little further. Always do your exercises with a slow, smooth motion.

Try to plan your exercise program during a part of the day when you have the least pain and stiffness and when you aren't tired. Two moderate exercise periods are better than one strenuous one.

You may experience some joint pain with your exercises. Pain is nature's way of telling us to slow down before an injury occurs. So if it hurts, slow down. Too much can be as bad as not enough! To help keep pain to a minimum, use heat to relax your joints before you exercise. A warm tub or shower or a heating pad is great for helping you reduce stiffness.

SOME EXERCISE BENEFITS
- *Keeps you flexible*
- *Strengthens your muscles*
- *Gives you more energy*
- *Relieves arthritis pain*

SOME EXERCISE CAUTIONS
- *Go slow - don't push*
- *Increase gradually*
- *Have a regular program*
- *Listen to your body*

While over 100 different kinds of arthritis have been identified, there are four types that occur most frequently.

	TYPE			
	Osteoarthritis	Rheumatoid Arthritis	Gout	Ankylosing Spondylitis
Cause	Breakdown of cartilage in joint	Inflammation of the mem-brane in joint	Build-up of minerals, usually uric acid crystals in the joint fluid	Inflammation of ligament at a joint of the spine
Symptoms	Pain, stiffness and swelling of joint	Pain, stiffness and swelling of joint. Fever.	Pain, stiffness and swelling, commonly of the big toe	Pain and stiff-ness of the spine
Comments	Most common type for both women and men between the ages of 45-90	Occurs most often in mid-dle age, more common in women	Condition may be aggra-vated by foods high in "pur-ines" such as organ meats or by alcoholic beverages	Most common in young men but results of the illness (stiff back) can last a life-time

Arthritis can be a real pain, but try not to let it get you down or keep you from doing what you want to do. You might have to modify some of your activities to accommodate your arthritis, but that may not be all bad. Did you know that Grandma Moses took up painting at the age of 76 because her arthritis made it too painful to continue with her needle-work? She first showed her paintings when she was 80, was an instant success, and continued to paint until she was over 100 years old.

BASIC TREATMENT PLAN FOR ARTHRITIS

Rest	• Get plenty of rest (8-12 hours/night and 1-2 hours/day)
Exercise	• Get plenty of exercise. Do activities that emphasize slow, gradual movement of all the joints: - Try the exercises on pages 9-22. - Walk short distances two to three times daily. - Water exercises, including swimming, are excellent for the joints. - Avoid jarring activities such as jogging, jumping, etc.
Breathing	• Use Roll Breathing (page 34) to help you relax and ease the discomfort of arthritis.
Flare-Ups	• During flare-ups apply heat, cold or both — whichever feels the best.
Shoes	• Do not wear high-heeled shoes, pointed-toe shoes, sandals, slippers or thongs. These cause discomfort by putting undue stress on joints. See shoe recommendation on page 20.
Call Doctor If:	• Call your doctor if: - A flare-up lasts more than six weeks. - The pain is severe or sharp. - The arthritis pain is accompanied by a fever. - Your home remedies do not seem to be working.
Medications	• Discuss all arthritis medications with your doctor and pharmacist including the use of aspirin.

References

Arthritis, a Comprehensive Guide, James F. Fries, M.D., Addison-Wesley Publishing Co., 1979

Take Care of Yourself, D.M. Vickery, M.D. and James F. Fries, M.D., Addison-Wesley Publishing Co., 1978

The Doctors Guide to Growing Older, Sandor A. Friedman, M.D., Francis U. Steenhaber, M.D., and Abraham H. Lass, New American Library, 1980

To Your Good Health, Robert J. Skiest, R.M., Chicago Review Press, 1980

THE ILLS OF PILLS

When used appropriately, medicines can be of great help in controlling infections, easing pain, and managing certain types of chronic illness. When used inappropriately or to excess, they may cause physical injury, mental confusion, personality change, or even death, and may alter the effects of other medicines you take. The safe use of medicines requires a well-informed consumer: **YOU!**

Most medicines act differently in an older body than they do in a younger person's body. This is mostly due to the normal changes that occur in your body as you age.

WHAT HAPPENS TO YOUR BODY'S SYSTEMS AS YOU GROW OLDER?

As you go from age 21 to age 65...

STOMACH - Absorption drops 25% - drug is exposed to stomach acid longer.

HEART - Circulation and heart output drops 1% per year. Drug stays in blood stream longer.

KIDNEYS - Excretion of the drug from the body drops 6% every 10 years. Less drug is excreted in urine, more stays in body.

LIVER - Holds out, as long as everything is in moderation.

BODY - Total number of cells drops 40%. Weight drops, increasing the drug concentration in the body.

Basically, medicines can be divided into two main categories: those which can be purchased without a doctor's prescription (called Over-The-Counter medicines), and those which must be prescribed by a doctor. People aged 65 or older take 25% of all prescription medicines.

If you take medicines, be sure you know **what** you are taking, **why** you take it, and **how long** you will be taking it. What **effects** the medicine can be expected to have on you is also important to know.

Since two or more medications taken at the same time can sometimes react with each other and cause problems, it's a good idea to check with your pharmacist if you add a new medicine or are unsure about possible drug interactions. Pharmacists are experts in both prescription and Over-The-Counter medicines and are your best resource for drug information.

YOUR PHARMACIST WILL:

1. *Explain the benefits and dangers of specific medicines.*
2. *Help you select non-prescription drugs.*
3. *Keep a record of all your drugs and allergies.*
4. *Tell you if all your drugs will go together.*
5. *Tell you if a possible drug problem exists.*

The Drug-Taker's Checklist

Each time a drug is prescribed, record all important information about it in your Home Health Records (see example below) and consider the following questions:

Questions to Consider

- What are the expected effects?
- When and how do I take it?
- How long do I take it?
- Can I get refills?
- Will other drugs affect it?
- Is there a generic equivalent?
- How should it be stored?
- Under what circumstances should I become concerned about side effects or adverse reactions?
- What is the expiration date?

HOME HEALTH RECORD

Name of Drug: _____

Date Prescribed: _____

Doctor's Name: _____

Prescribed for What? _____

_____

Color/Shape/Strength: _____

_____

Directions: _____

_____

_____

Other Information: _____

_____

DRUG INTERACTION CHART

This Drug	Taken For	Can React With	To Cause
Aspirin	Reduction of pain, fever and swelling	Alcohol	Bleeding from the stomach lining
		Food	Delayed pain relief
Tylenol	Reduction of pain, fever and swelling	Food	Delayed pain relief
Darvon	Reduction of pain, fever and swelling	Food	Delayed pain relief
Antacids	Indigestion, stomach ulcers	Tetracycline (Achromycin, Declomycin, Menocin, Terramycin, Vebromycin)	Inactivates the tetracycline so infection may continue
		Iron Preparations	Inactivates the iron so anemia may continue
Antihistamines	Allergies	Alcohol	Drowsiness & decreased mental alertness
Flagyl	Infections	Alcohol	Headache, vomiting, rapid heartbeat, blurred vision
Penicillin/Ampicillin	Infections	Food Fruit juices	Reduces absorption of penicillin in bloodstream

This Drug	Taken For	Can React With	To Cause
Tetracycline	Infections	Milk & dairy products	Reduces absorption of tetracycline in bloodstream
Anti-coagulants: "Blood Thinners", Coumadin, Pan Warfin	Prevention of blood clots	Aspirin	Bruises, bleeding from digestive or urinary tract
		Some antibiotics (Flagyl, Sulfa, Gantrisin, Bactrin, Thiosulfil)	Bruises, bleeding from digestive or urinary tract
		Some sleeping pills (Luminal, Amytal, Seconal, Barbital, Tuinal)	Bruises, bleeding from digestive or urinary tract
		Foods high in Vitamin K (asparagus, broccoli, cabbage, beef liver, lettuce, spinach, watercress)	Decreased effectiveness of anticoagulant
Lomotil	Control of diarrhea	Some tranquilizers (Ativan, Tranxene, Librium, Valium, Serax, Vestran)	Increases the effect of the tranquilizers, sedatives and sleeping pills

This Drug	Taken For	Can React With	To Cause
Lomotil (cont'd)	Control of diarrhea	Some sedatives (Dalmane, Doriden, Noctec, Placidyl, Quaalude)	Same as above
		Some sleeping pills (Amytal, Barbital, Luminal, Nembutal, Seconal, Tuinal)	Same as above
Sleeping Pills: Amytal, Barbital, Luminal, Nembutal, Seconal, Tuinal, Dalmane, Doriden, Noctec, Placidyl, Quaalude	Relaxation or sleep	Alcohol	Extreme drowsiness, unconsciousness, coma, death
Tranquilizers: Ativan, Librium, Serax, Tranxene, Valium, Vestran	Relaxation or reduction of anxiety	Alcohol	Extreme drowsiness, unconsciousness, coma, death

Pharmacy References:

The People's Pharmacy-2, Joe Graedon, Avon Publishers, 1980
Physicians' Desk Reference (PDR)
Allen Frisk, R Ph, M.S.

97

YOU, SEXUALITY & AGING

Sexual activity in your later years is a healthy, vital part of a happy and fulfilling life style. Contrary to what you may have heard, people over 60 do not lose all interest in sexual activity. The need for close, warm bodily and emotional contact is a part of every human being, and it does not have to diminish with age. In fact, this warm contact should be encouraged with age.

Natural changes do take place that can affect sexual interest and capacity. The natural slowing down of the entire body that affects how you exercise and how you eat also affects sexual activities. But that doesn't mean you have to stop exercising or stop eating or stop sexual activity. It may mean making some changes to maximize comfort, satisfaction and emotional well-being. Below are lists of those basic physical changes related to sexuality that frequently occur in both men and women:

Common Physical Changes in Men

- The erection may be less hard with age.
- The ability to delay ejaculation for a longer period of time usually increases (this can be an advantage).
- It may take longer to get an erection.
- Semen release may be less forceful.
- It may take longer to achieve a second erection.

Tips for Men

- Sexual activity may be easier in the morning, since hormone levels are usually higher at this time.

- If you have trouble getting an erection, consider using the "stuffing technique." You or your partner places the flaccid penis right into the vagina. Usually, within a short time, the penis will become hard enough for sexual intercourse.
- Take more time for "sex play," including touching, holding and genital play.

Common Physical Changes in Women

- Most changes take place with the onset of menopause and are the result of lowered hormone levels.
- A thinning of the vaginal walls can cause an irritation during intercourse.
- Less lubrication (wetness) in the vagina can also make sexual intercourse uncomfortable.
- Contractions experienced during orgasm can sometimes become uncomfortable.
- It may take longer to become sexually aroused (excited).
- The orgasm can be somewhat shorter or less strong than it used to be.

Tips for Women

- Use an inexpensive vaginal cream or jelly (K-Y Jelly) for lubrication. It can be purchased over-the-counter at most drug stores.
- Discuss any irritations of the vaginal wall with your doctor. Prescription hormone creams are available to treat this situation.
- Take more time for "sex play."

Use It or Lose It

Just as exercise is the key to maintaining fitness, having some form of sex regularly is the best way of maintaining sexual capacity. The more regular your sexual activities are, the longer your sexual abilities will last.

Just as variety is the key to good nutrition, variation in sexual activity can often increase sexual enjoyment. The book, *The Joy of Sex,* by Alex Comfort, is full of healthy ideas to avoid boring and routine sex.

Facts About You, Your Health and Your Sexuality

- Illness or an operation does not have to put an end to your sexual activity. Seek advice from a counselor or a physician who will give you honest answers and realistic suggestions.

- Women who have had hysterectomies are still capable of full and satisfying sexual lives.

- There are a number of medications including alcohol, tranquilizers, antidepressants and some antihypertensives that may adversely affect sexual activity. This is one of the first issues you should discuss with your physician if a sexual problem develops.

- Colostomies, mastectomies and other operations that involve physical changes need not put an end to sexual activities. These surgeries frequently require the individual and his/her partner to emotionally work through the adjustment.

- If your changed appearance or health condition causes you sad feelings and thus causes you to give up sex, consider consulting a qualified therapist who can help you work around these feelings.

- People with heart conditions can enjoy full, satisfying sexual lives, without fear of a sudden heart attack or stroke during sexual activity. Following a heart attack most physicians recommend a brief period of abstention (8-14 weeks).

(The material on sexuality was adapted from: Mona Wasow, *Sexuality and Aging* booklet, 1976, 1120 Edgehill Dr., Madison, WI 53705.)

CONTROLLING URINATION IN WOMEN

Here is a set of exercises to help women with the problem of controlling urination. The exercises are designed to strengthen the muscles that control urination. (Adapted from Kegel Method.)

The Exercises:

1. The first step is to locate the muscles that control urination. This is done by consciously stopping the flow of urine and then starting the flow again. It might take several attempts to locate the muscles to be exercised.

2. Now that you have found the muscles, tighten those muscles, hold them, count to three, and relax.

3. Now rapidly tighten and relax the muscles.

4. The next step of the exercise involves the stomach (abdominal) muscles. Combine the previous exercise with a pulling of the muscles that control the area between the vagina and rectum and then include the pulling of the stomach (abdominal) muscles.

Breathe naturally throughout the exercise period.

Do each exercise 10 times, then gradually increase the number daily as tolerated.

The exercises are to be practiced a minimum of **five** times a day. The exercises can be practiced while you go about your daily activities. Keep at it and in a few weeks you will probably notice great improvement in controlling urination.

Adapted from *Exercises for Women* by Helen Hallgren, R.N., Ph.N., County of Marin Senior Health Project.

PREVENTING OSTEOPOROSIS

For a woman past menopause, one of the greatest risks to the quality of life is that of breaking certain bones, especially your spine or hip. Osteoporosis is an illness which greatly reduces bone strength in about twenty-five percent of women over sixty years of age and causes an estimated 1.3 million fractures per year. Osteoporosis is much less common and severe in men.

Most women over fifty lose about one half of one percent of bone mass per year. Thus, by age ninety, their bone mass has dropped about twenty percent, not enough to cause problems. However, in the woman suffering from osteoporosis, the loss could be two to four times higher. When a woman's bone loss reaches thirty percent of the original mass, the condition is called clinical osteoporosis. For such a woman, a fall, blow, or lifting action that would not bruise or strain the average person can easily cause one or more bones to break.

Post-menopausal women concerned about bone loss and fractures can take several steps to avoid, reduce, or delay the problem.

Increase Calcium

The average American gets about 500 milligrams (mg) of calcium per day. Because calcium is absorbed more slowly by older women, a daily intake of 1,500 mg is recommended. The extra 1,000 mg needed can be obtained either by a large increase in dairy products (a quart of skim milk would add 1,100 mg of calcium and only 350 calories), or by taking a calcium supplement. Calcium carbonate seems to be the best and least expensive supplement, with a 1,000 mg table yielding 400 mg of calcium. Two-and-a-half, 1,000 mg tablets are needed to get 1,000 mg of calcium. If you take more than one tablet, space them out over the day with one before bedtime because calcium is absorbed slowly. Take them between meals with a small amount of milk or yogurt; the vitamin D and lactose in dairy products aid calcium absorption. Some supplements also contain vitamin D and lactose.

Increase Regular Exercise

Moderate weight-bearing exercise, such as walking, is believed to reduce bone loss. For older women, it is particularly important to start slowly and increase exercise only gradually.

Estrogen Therapy

The most effective method of stopping bone loss immediately after menopause is estrogen relacement therapy. However, because estrogen therapy is suspected of increasing cancer risks, many physicians and patients prefer to reserve estrogen therapy for those with a high chance of developing serious osteoporosis. Estrogen therapy may not help prevent osteoporosis unless begun shortly after menopause.

References

The Doctors Guide to Growing Older, Sandor A. Friedman, M.D., Francis U. Steenhaber, M.D., and Abraham H. Lass, New American Library, 1980

Arthritis, a Comprehensive Guide, James F. Fries, M.D., Addison-Wesley Publishing Co., 1979

Healthwise Handbook, Donald W. Kemper, Kathleen McIntosh Tinker, and Toni M. Roberts, Joslyn & Morris, Fourth Edition, 1984

Treat Your Own Back, Robin McKenzie, Wright and Carman Ltd., New Zealand, Reprinted 1983

To Your Good Health, Robert J. Skeist, R.N., Chicago Review Press, 1980

Take Care of Yourself, D.M. Vickery, M.D., and James F. Fries, M.D., Addison-Wesley Publishing Co., 1976

Chapter 5
HEALTH CARE
Personal Management

> The two greatest weaknesses in our health care system are that:
>
> 1. we expect too much from it, and
> 2. we expect too little from ourselves.

This chapter describes how you can better manage your use of professional health care services. It suggests that you can take a more **active** role in the decisions that affect your health care and your health.

On the one hand, it is easy to rely on our doctors. Most are well-trained, experienced and concerned about our health. They work daily with the sophisticated equipment and complex terminology that may be strange and confusing to us. They also understand the workings of the human body and the ways that illness affects it. It would be foolish indeed to ignore such a resource.

On the other hand, no physician can know all that you know about yourself and what is important to you. Most medical decisions require some judgment about whether the expected benefits are worth the cost and the possible risks. After your doctor has given you his medical opinion and answered your questions, the treatment decision should be made by you.

In this chapter you will learn how to choose a doctor you can truly work with. If you don't want to change to another doctor, consider **changing** your doctor. Health professionals can learn from your actions and attitudes, especially if you are positive and well-prepared. You will learn how to improve your communication with doctors and nurses so that both you and they benefit. Your rights and responsibilities in the doctor-patient relationship will be highlighted. Finally, you will learn useful tips for saving money on hospital and insurance bills.

In 1980 the cost of medical care for those 65 and over exceeded $3,000 per person, three times that of the overall per capita health care cost. To the extent that $3,000 a year can prolong active, enjoyable and productive living, the cost can either be a bargain or a waste of money. Whether or not you get your money's worth from the health care you receive depends in large measure on what part you play as the leader of your own health care team.

A PARTNERSHIP FOR HEALTH

You and Your Doctor
Although what you do for yourself affects your health most, your doctor can become one of your most important health resources. How you choose a doctor, what you expect from him or her, and how much you are willing to work on your health care team, will largely determine how much help your doctor can provide. Each one of us is ultimately responsible for our own health. Your doctor can advise you, but you must make the decision.

Finding Your Marcus Welby
Here are some tips for finding a doctor you can work with:
1. Start with recommendations from friends.
2. Call the doctor's office to learn:
   - Specific training or interest in geriatrics
   - Fee schedule
   - Appointment backlog
   - On call coverage
   - Phone calls
   - Home visits
   - Accepting Medicare patients
   - Help in filing Medicare and insurance forms
   - Location and office hours
3. Ask another doctor or health professional for recommendations.
4. Send a letter to the doctor or doctors you are considering. (See sample next page.)
5. Make an appointment to interview the doctor and set up your file. (You will probably be charged — ask how much first.) A sample interview form is provided.
6. If you have moved or are planning to move to a new area, ask your present physician if he/she has contacts in your new location.
7. Ask your former physician to transfer your medical records to your new physician.

SAMPLE LETTER

Dear Dr. _____:

    I am currently seeking a primary care doctor in the _____
(your town)

area. I am _____ years old and have the following health concerns:

(List major health problems.)

    I do try to eat well, exercise and relax to maintain my health as best I can.

    You have been recommended to me as a doctor who can both treat my illnesses and help me learn what more I might do for myself to prevent or treat health problems. If you are able to take me as a patient, I would like to schedule a short visit to meet you and fill out necessary forms. Please let me know if there will be a charge for such a visit.

    I look forward to your reply.

Sincerely,

Interviewing the Doctor

1. Ask if he/she minds if you ask questions to learn how you might help yourself.
2. Ask if he/she has any special training or interest in geriatric medicine.
3. Ask how much he/she thinks a person your age should exercise and modify eating habits.
4. Ask if he/she devotes time to patient education during office visits.

    These are only suggested questions. Make up your own to reflect your interests and needs. Decide exactly what you expect from your doctor and then find one who shares these same interests.

Communicating with Your Doctor

    Communication is the key in helping your doctor help you. You should never leave a health professional's office not knowing: what's wrong with you in terms you can understand, what treatment is recommended, and what you can do at home to speed the healing process or prevent it from happening again.

    One easy way to help you communicate with your doctor is to be **prepared.** The Ask-The-Doctor List (page 106), if used before, during, and after your visit or phone call, will help you prepare and will help your doctor understand exactly what you want. Usually a physician will be pleased to see you taking such an active interest in your health and well-being. This activity can go a long way toward improving communication with your doctor.

Be Direct and Assertive:
- Write your questions down.
- Be persistent until you can explain the answers back to your doctor.
- Encourage the doctor to draw a picture.
- Write it down.
- Before you leave, make sure you know exactly what you are supposed to do at home.
- If you decide you don't want to or can't follow a suggestion/medication, tell your doctor and ask for alternatives.
- If you agree to take a medication, be sure you know when, how, how much and why you're taking it. (See page 93.)
- Agree on when you should phone or come back for a follow-up visit and ask for danger signals to watch out for.
- Be polite. Chances are, your doctor is just as interested as you are in having you understand as much as you can.

(Sometimes it helps to practice one of the breathing exercises in the relaxation chapter to calm you down before you visit the doctor.)

THE ASK-THE-DOCTOR LIST

Before the visit, complete this part yourself:
1. Why am I going to the doctor? (the main reason)
_____
2. Is there anything else that worries me about my health?
____ No   ____ Yes (List) _____
3. What do I expect the doctor to do for me today? (in 10 words or less)
_____

During the visit, complete with help of doctor:
1. What is the diagnosis? _____
2. How did I get it and how can I prevent it next time? _____
_____
3. Are there any helpful patient education materials available for the condition? (Describe) _____
4. Are there any medications for me to take?
____ No   ____ Yes (Describe) _____
5. Are there any special instructions, concerns, or possible side effects I

need to know about the medicine?

___ No ___ Yes (Describe) _____

After the visit, complete with help of doctor or nurse:

1. Am I to return for another visit? ___ No ___ Yes
   When? _____
2. What should I do at home?
   ___ Activity _____
   ___ Treatments _____
   ___ Precautions _____
3. Am I to phone in for test results? ___ No ___ Yes
   When? _____
4. What danger signs should I look for? _____
5. Should I report back to the doctor or nurse by phone for any reason?
   ___ No ___ Yes When? _____

Adapted from *How To Be Your Own Doctor (Sometimes)* by Keith Sehnert, M.D.

YOUR RIGHTS AND RESPONSIBILITIES WITH YOUR DOCTOR

YOU HAVE A RIGHT	*YOU HAVE A RESPONSIBILITY*
• *To be spoken to in terms you* **understand.** • *To be told what's wrong when you ask.* • *To know the benefits and risks of any treatment, and its alternatives.* • *To know the benefits and side effects of any drug prescribed.* • *To know how much a service will cost and to receive an itemized bill.* • *To a second opinion.* • *To make all treatment decisions.* • *To refuse any medical procedure.*	• *To accurately describe your symptoms.* • *To ask about anything you don't understand (written questions help).* • *To bring a list of your medications.* • *To be honest about your treatment plans.* • *To ask what you can do to reduce the problem.* • *To pay your bill when due or make special credit arrangements.* • *To reschedule in advance any appointment you can't keep.*

YOU CAN SAVE ON HOSPITAL BILLS

Hospital services are both valuable and expensive. Sometimes they are risky, too. Generally, you are better off to stay in a hospital only for the least amount of time needed for your treatment.

More is not always better in health care. Who with a healthy heart would want a heart transplant, even if it were free? No one would, because there are risks to heart surgery. Well, there are risks involved in other medical treatments, too. So if you don't absolutely need the treatment, consider avoiding the risk.

Eliminating unnecessary hospital care also saves money, both for you and for Medicare or your insurers. That's important because high hospital costs could otherwise cause your hospital benefits to go down.

By working with your physician you can usually reduce both the cost and the risks of hospitalization.

Ways to Save — BEFORE You Get to the Hospital

1. Second Opinion for Non-Emergency Surgery
Your doctor should tell you exactly why you need to go to the hospital. If you still aren't sure surgery or hospitalization is needed, ask for a second opinion. Your doctor will then send you and your records to another physician to reassess if hospitalization and/or surgery is needed. Most doctors welcome requests by their patients for second opinions. Gall bladder operations, hysterectomies, hernia repairs, back surgery, and cataract operations are often non-emergency procedures for which a second opinion is sometimes helpful.

2. Pre-Admission Testing
If you must be hospitalized, ask your doctor if the routine tests that will be necessary can be done on an outpatient basis. This can often reduce your hospital stay by at least one day.

3. Hospitalization for Testing Only
Some medical testing requires that you strictly control your diet and activity for 12 hours or more before the test. Physicians will sometimes hospitalize a person to be sure the diet controls are met before a test is run. By agreeing to limit your own diet you may avoid having to be hospitalized for testing.

4. Same Day Surgery
If you must have surgery, ask if it can be done just as safely in your

doctor's office, or on an outpatient basis in the hospital. Many types of surgery can be handled this way, allowing you to return home the same day. Foot and hand surgery, hernia operations, cyst removals, breast biopsies and D & C's are often done on a same day basis.

5. Emergency Room Use

Use self care or your physician, not the hospital emergency room for routine problems. Emergency rooms are best kept for true emergencies. If your problem is not an emergency, you can expect to wait longer and to be charged more at the emergency room than at a doctor's office.

6. Stay Healthy

Of course the best way to avoid hospital costs is to stay healthy, By following the **GROWING YOUNGER** guidelines for eating, exercise and relaxation, you should avoid much illness and hospitalization.

Ways to Save — AFTER You Are in the Hospital

1. Understand Why

If you do not understand the reason for a laboratory test, x-ray test, or treatment ask for a clear explanation of the benefits and the probable consequences of not doing it. You always have the right to say no. If you feel you are not being treated with dignity by the hospital staff, speak to the nursing supervisor or to your doctor about it.

2. Ask How Much

When your doctor orders a test or special service, ask what it will cost. Often doctors don't know the cost of services and may decide that a test or service really isn't needed when they learn the cost.

3. Learn What You Can Do

While you are in the hospital, learn what you can do to help yourself recover faster and to prevent future problems. Ask for educational materials about your health concerns.

4. Patient-Kept Records

If you feel up to it, try to keep your own records of drugs, tests, physician visits and treatments received at the hospital. You can later compare your record with the hospital bill for accuracy. Of course it is practically impossible to record every little service and supply received but by keeping track of what you can, you will be better able to spot both billing and health care errors before they become serious.

5. Going Home Arrangements

Arrange for your family or friends to assist you after you go home. If you tell your doctor that you want to go home as soon as possible and that you will be cared for adequately, you might be able to reduce your hospital stay.

HOW TO REQUEST MEDICARE PAYMENTS

Part "A" - Hospital Insurance (Hospital in-patient care, extended care, home health services)

Always ask for a copy of your itemized bill when you leave the hospital so you can check it for possible mistakes while it is fresh in your mind. You will not know how much of the bill you will have to pay for 4 to 8 weeks.

The hospital or agency will bill Medicare directly. Four to 8 weeks later you will receive a "Medicare Benefits Records" with an explanation of how much of the bill Medicare has paid.

Then, **you will be billed** by the hospital or agency for the deductible, co-insurance, and other services not paid for by Medicare. If you can't pay this bill right away, call the hospital billing office and arrange for a payment plan.

Part "B" - Medical Insurance (Doctor services, medical equipment, home health services, hospital out-patient services)

There are two methods of Part "B" payment, depending on whether your doctor agrees to accept the Medicare-allowed amount as his or her total fee.

1. Assignment Method (works just like Part "A")
Ask your doctor if he accepts assignment of Medicare payments. If he does:
   a. You complete and sign the **top half** of the "Request For Medicare Payment Form" (HCFA-1490) at the time of your visit to the doctor.

   b. The doctor will then bill Medicare directly.

   c. About 4 to 6 weeks later you should receive an "Explanation Of Medicare Benefits" (EOMB) telling you how much Medicare has paid. Take time to read it carefully - each section has information about the payment made.

   d. Then you will be billed by the doctor for any deductibles, co-insurance or non-covered services that Medicare does not pay. (You should have

110

an itemized bill from your doctor, too, for your own review and records.

2. Non-Assignment Method

If your doctor does not accept assignment, you will be responsible for submitting the claim form to Medicare and for paying the balance of the bill not paid by Medicare.

a. You complete the top half of form HCFA-1490 and ask your doctor to give you an itemized bill which clearly shows:

- **Diagnosis**
- **Description, date** and **cost** of each service (see box below)
- The **name** of the person that provided each service.

b. Mail the request form and the bill to the Medicare Insurance Administrator. Call the nearest Social Security office for name and address.

GET YOUR FAIR SHARE!

*Please note that if medical services are not described fully, Medicare always assumes the **lowest priced service**. Be sure your doctor gives you a full description of the **diagnosis** and **service**. If you question the amount paid, call your Social Security office.*

Example: The price of an office visit to the same physician may vary from $15 to $50, depending on the length of the visit.

Limited Visit	$15
Regular Visit	$35
Extended Visit	$50

If you put on the claim form that the service was an "office visit," Medicare will assume that it was the limited visit and base their payment on that. **BE SPECIFIC!**

If this happens to you, feel free to appeal by asking for a review. Provide all the information that you can.

SUPPLEMENTAL INSURANCE

A basic Medicare supplement policy should pay your deductible and co-insurance costs. It can also offer additional hospital, skilled nursing, and home health coverage. One **good** policy is better than several. Coordination-of-benefits procedures may mean that you will only collect on one supplemental policy anyway.

Single disease policies, like cancer insurance, should be examined very carefully.

First of all, Medicare covers much of the care needed by people with cancer and other diseases covered by a specified disease policy.

Often cancer insurance does not pay or pays far less than expected when another insurer, such as Medicare, is covering the same costs.

Secondly, many of these policies have very restrictive conditions regarding the type of treatment covered and in what types of facilities covered treatment can be reimbursed.

Thirdly, many of these policies have low maximum payment amounts which are quickly exhausted in the event of a long treatment period.

Don't be pushed into buying until you have thought it over carefully. You have 10 days from the time you receive a policy in which to read it carefully and reject it if it does not meet your expectations.

Usual Procedure for Submitting Claims - Supplemental Insurance

1. Get **2** extra copies made of the doctor's bill.
2. Get a Claim Form from your insurance company.
3. Wait until you have received your "Explanation of Medicare Benefits" (EOMB).
4. Send the Claim Form, the bill and the EOMB to your insurance company.

Chapter 6
RECORDS
Your Health Records

More than any other tool, your own health records can help you take greater responsibility for your health.

- **Home Records Help You When You Are Well:**
  - By showing you how you have improved
  - By pointing out backslides
  - By focusing on your personal risk factors

- **Home Records Help When You Are Ill:**
  - By organizing your observation of symptoms
  - By "remembering" information from the past
  - By building your skills and confidence
  - By improving your communication with your doctor

Complete these forms as soon as you can and add to them whenever you have new health information. Add blank paper if you need more space. You should take your record with you whenever you visit a health professional.

GROWING YOUNGER PROGRESS SHEET

If you improve your eating, relaxation and exercise habits, you should begin to see the changes in your body. By periodically adding to your progress sheet, you will be able to see just how much you are improving.

FAMILY HISTORY

Many diseases are hereditary. If you have a complete family history of all blood relatives, then your health professional may more easily diagnose a particular disease that you have. You will also be able to see trends in your family tree toward certain ailments that you may be able to avoid. For example, if parents, aunts or uncles died of heart disease, you should consider that you have a high risk for an attack and take appropriate precautions.

RECORD OF HEALTH PROFESSIONALS

Occasionally, your present health professional may wish to confer with health professionals you visited in the past. This form, properly completed, would then be useful.

DRUG INVENTORY

Each time you purchase a drug, whether by prescription or over-the-counter, record the drug name, date of purchase, etc., in the appropriate column. Periodically glance at the record and discard and replace any out-of-date drugs. This form will have most value if you write down every drug or medication used. That way any possible ill effects from drug interaction can be quickly traced. The last column is reserved for listing any adverse reactions to the drug (ADR), whether you think it worked well or poorly, and other general comments.

Show this record to your doctor or pharmacist if you want assistance in reviewing your drugs.

RECORD OF ILLNESSES, ACCIDENTS, AND SURGERIES

A record of illness can also be helpful to you. You may recognize that you have an abnormal number of colds each year and suspect an allergy. Records of accidents and surgeries can be useful for insurance purposes. Comments can include any home treatments given, how long the treatment lasted, and names of health professionals consulted, if any.

DENTAL RECORDS

If this form is kept up-to-date you can readily see when you last had your teeth checked or cleaned to determine your next appointment. It will also be useful to see if you are having more fillings, in which case you would want to start flossing and brushing more regularly.

Denture wearers should have an examination by a dentist at least once a year.

SELF-CARE EXAM

This form has been explained in detail beginning on page 57 of Chapter 4.

Family History

Name _____

Names of Family Members	If Deceased, Age and Cause	Diseases such as diabetes, heart disease, cancer, allergies, hypertension, alcoholism, ulcers, stroke, mental illness, epilepsy, etc.
Great-Grandparents		
Grandparents		
Aunts and Uncles		
Parents		
Brothers and Sisters		
Children		

115

RECORD OF HEALTH PROFESSIONALS

Health Professional's Name and Address	Specialty	Office Phone and Hours	Dates Started and Ended	Comments

RECORD OF HEALTH PROFESSIONALS

(Continued)

Health Professional's Name and Address	Specialty	Office Phone and Hours	Dates Started and Ended	Comments

Drug Inventory

DRUG	PURPOSE/PERSON	RX NO.	COST	INSTRUCTIONS	DATE PURCH.	EXPIR. DATE	POSSIBLE SIDE EFFECTS	USE EFFECT Adverse Drug Reaction (if any)

Drug Inventory
(Continued)

DRUG	PURPOSE/PERSON	RX NO.	COST	INSTRUCTIONS	DATE PURCH.	EXPIR. DATE	POSSIBLE SIDE EFFECTS	USE, EFFECT Adverse Drug Reaction [if any]

RECORD OF ILLNESSES, ACCIDENTS AND SURGERIES

Add to this record each time you are ill or go to your doctor.

Name _____

Date	Description	Health Professional	Comments

RECORD OF ILLNESSES,
ACCIDENTS AND SURGERIES
(Continued)

Name _____

Date	Description	Health Professional	Comments

HOME HEALTH CARE EXAM

Date _____ Name _____

Time of day _____

VITAL SIGNS

Height	Weight

Temperature
   Rectal   Oral
	Pulse
	     Beats per minute? Regular?

Respiration Breaths per minute?	Blood Pressure

Reason for physical exam _____

Overall impression, comments _____

_____

Mental health observations _____

Skin	Skull, hair, scalp
Eyes Pupil constriction	Nose
Ears Hearing	Mouth, teeth

HOME HEALTH CARE EXAM

(Continued)

Throat	Neck, lymph nodes Chin to chest
Chest, breasts	Spine
Abdomen	Genitals
Anus Bowel movements	Legs and arms
Hands, nails	Feet, nails
Chest, lungs, heart sounds	
Adult women (over 18) Breast	

Additional comments: _____

_____

_____

_____

DENTAL RECORD

Name _____

Date	Name of Professional	Comments

Index